PLAYS BY TONY KUSHNER

357 W 20th St., NY NY 10011
212 627-1055

First printing: March 1992
ISBN: 0-88145-102-9

Book design: Marie Donovan
Word processing: WordMarc Composer Plus
Typographic controls: Xerox Ventura Publisher 2.0 PE
Typeface: Palatino
Printed on recycled acid-free paper, and bound in the USA.

CONTENTS

ABOUT THE AUTHOR

Tony Kushner's first play, A BRIGHT ROOM CALLED DAY, was first produced in New York by Heat & Light Co., Inc.; in San Francisco, Chicago, London, and at the New York Shakespeare Festival's Public Theater. His adaptation of Corneille's THE ILLUSION has been produced at theaters around the country, including New York Theater Workshop, Hartford Stage, the Los Angeles Theater Center, and Berkeley Repertory Theater; and is currently being adapted for film for Universal Studios.

Tony Kushner also translated and adapted Goethe's STELLA, and co-authored, with Ariel Dorfman, the stage adaptation of Mr Dorfman's WIDOWS. His new two-part play, ANGELS IN AMERICA, was commissioned by longtime collaborator Oskar Eustis and the Eureka Theater through a special projects grant from the NEA. The first part, MILLENNIUM APPROACHES, was a winner of a 1990 Fund For New American Plays/Kennedy Center award, and the 1991 Joseph Kesselring Award; it was premiered at the Eureka in the summer of 1991; it will be seen in the winter of 1991-92 at the National Theater in London. The world premiere of the entire two-evening work is scheduled for the summer of 1992 at the Mark Taper Forum.

Mr Kushner is currently playwright-in-residence at Julliard School of Drama. He has received playwriting and directing fellowships from NYSCA, NYFA, and the NEA, a Princess Grace Foundation Theater Award, and a 1990 Whiting Foundation Writers Award. Kushner was born in Manhattan in 1956, and grew up in Lake Charles, Louisiana. He has a BA from Columbia University and an MFA in directing from NYU, where he studied with Carl Weber. He lives in Brooklyn.

A BRIGHT ROOM
CALLED DAY

A BRIGHT ROOM CALLED DAY

A BRIGHT ROOM CALLED DAY was first presented by Heat & Light Co in a workshop production at Theatre 22 in New York City in April 1985, with the following cast and creative contributors:

AGNES EGGLING .... Priscilla Stampa
BAZ .... Stephen Spinella
PAULINKA ERDNUSS .... Alexandra Rambusch
ANNABELLA GOTCHLING .... Maria Makis
VEALTNINC HUSZ .... Peter Guttmacher
ROSA MALEK .... Kimberly Flynn
EMIL TRAUM .... Jonathan Rosenberg
ZILLAH .... Roberta Levine
ZACHARY* .... Michael Mayer
DIE ALTE .... Theresa Reeves
AH* .... Tracy Martin
GOTTFRIED SWETTS .... David Warshofsky

*Characters died in the rewrites.

Director .... Tony Kushner
Production design .... Steven Rosen and Tony Kushner

The play premiered in San Francisco at the Eureka Theatre in October 1987. Oskar Eustis directed the following cast: Sigrid Wurschmidt, Jeff King, Carmalita Fuentes, Abigail Van Alyn, Michael McShane, Ann Houle, Lorri Holt, Jaime Sempre, and David Warshofsky.

It was most recently produced at the Public Theatre by Joseph Papp's New York Shakespeare Festival in January 1991. Michael Greif directed the following cast: Frances Conroy, Henry Stram, Ellen McLaughlin, Joan MacIntosh, Olek Krupa, Angie Phillips, Kenneth L. Marks, Marian Seldes, and Frank Raiter.

The play benefitted immeasurably from the editing and dramaturgical advice provided by Kimberly Flynn, Carl Weber, Ellen McLaughlin, and Oskar Eustis. Through frequent discussion with Oskar Eustis the shape of the play has changed substantially since its first incarnation; this version incorporates many of his structural ideas and suggestions.

Thanks also to Mark Bronnenberg for his keen eye and loving support.

A BRIGHT ROOM CALLED DAY is for Carl Weber, teacher, mentor, and friend; for Kimberly Flynn, a true and triumphant heroine in the face of great adversity; and is dedicated to the memory of Florence Kushner: Zeicher tzadikah livrachah.

A BRIEF HISTORICAL NOTE

A parliamentary government was established in Germany in 1918 following the human and military disaster of World War I. The Weimar Republic was a constitutional democracy, Germany's first experiment with the form, in which authority was divided between an elected president, an elected national parliament (the Reichstag), regional parliaments, and a chancellor (roughly equivalent to a prime minister, appointed by the president to shape and oversee workable parliamentary coalitions). The Republic survived attempts by the German Army High Command to seize power, as well as a failed communist revolution in 1919 and several aborted fascist coups during the twenties.

For most of its existence, the Weimar government was marked by its inability to arrive at stable coalitions. The Reichstag was stalemated time and again, and the President repeatedly dissolved it. While the parties of the Right moved closer to cooperation and political solidarity, the main powers of the German Left, the gigantic Social-Democratic Party (SPD) and the German Communist Party (KPD), were entirely unable to form a united front to stop the rise of fascism. Instead, the SPD wasted critical time and energy seeking common ground with the Right, while the KPD's energies were increasingly strangled by interference from the Comintern, Moscow's international communist directorate.

The National Socialist German Workers' Party (the Nazis) grew from political obscurity to prominence in the early 1930s. In 1932 they became the largest voting bloc in the Reichstag, having received 37.5% of the popular vote in the July parliamentary elections. Although their popularity began to decline immediately after this, and though the KPD's popularity began concurrently to rise, the Nazis were able, through the support of the conservative and

Catholic center parties, the military and major industrialists, to secure from aging President Hindenburg the appointment of their leader, Adolf Hitler, to the post of Chancellor of the German Reich.

CHARACTERS

AGNES EGGLING: Mid- to late-thirties; preferably heavyset. Bit player/character actress in the German film industry.

GREGOR BAZWALD (BAZ): Early- to mid-thirties. Homosexual who works for the Berlin Institute for Human Sexuality.

PAULINKA ERDNUSS: Mid-thirties, but looks a little younger. Actress in the German film industry; a featured player on her way to becoming a minor star.

ANNABELLA GOTCHLING: Mid-forties. Communist artist and graphic designer.

VEALTNINC HUSZ: Mid-forties. Cinematographer. Hungarian exile. Missing an eye, he wears spectacles with one lens blackened.

ROSA MALEK: Mid- to late-twenties. Minor functionary of the KPD (Kommunistische Partei Deutschlands).

EMIL TRAUM: Mid- to late-twenties. Slightly higher-ranking functionary of the KPD.

DIE ALTE: A woman, very old but hard to tell how old— somewhere between seventy and dead-for-twenty years. White face and rotten teeth. Dressed in a nightgown, once white but now soiled and food-stained.

GOTTFRIED SWETTS: Ageless; when he looks good he could be thirty, when he looks bad he could be fifty (or more). Distinguished, handsome, blond, Aryan.

ZILLAH KATZ: Contemporary American Jewish woman. Thirties. BoHo/East Village New Wave with Anarcho-Punk tendencies.

ROLAND: In his twenties, born in East Germany back when there was such a thing. Now hanging out in what was formerly West Berlin. Speaks no English.

PRODUCTION NOTES

A BRIGHT ROOM CALLED DAY is set entirely in AGNES EGGLING's apartment, a small flat in a large nineteenth-century apartment building in a low-rent district in Berlin. The apartment has probably no more than three rooms. Only the main room is visible. It is cluttered, cozy, and has large windows. The set should be as uneasily realistic as the text is, and the apartment must be a room everyone would want to occupy. The ZILLAH interruptions take place in the apartment fifty-seven years later, and something—lights or an actual physical change in the set—should connote the transformations of time.

The slides are essential; the scene titles aren't meant to be printed or projected.

The photograph of the Nazi rally referred to in the stage directions and by ZILLAH in Act II is an actual photograph and can be obtained from the author.

About ZILLAH: ZILLAH is a character who exists in the present. She changes with the times, keeping her panic up-to-date, and has been doing so since her creation in deepest-midnight Reagan America. Each production of the play will require new material, the extent of the revisions determined by how far we've come (or how much lower we've sunk) since the circumstances of this most recent rewrite, during the year that saw the reunification of Germany and America's bloodthirsty misadventure begin in the Persian Gulf. The author will cheerfully supply new material, drawing appropriate parallels between contemporary and historical monsters and their monstrous acts, regardless of how superficially outrageous such comparisons may seem. To refuse to compare is to rob history of its power to inform present action.

"You know, upon our German stages,
Each man puts on just what he may;
So spare me not upon this day...
So in this narrow house of boarded space
Creation's fullest circle go to pace
And walk, with leisured speed, your spell
Past Heaven, through the Earth, to Hell."
Faust
(from the Prologue in *The Theatre*, Walter Arndt [trans.])

"The Republic had too much in common with its enemy; the spirit of
revenge for Versailles, the fear of communism... But above all the
Republic was aware of its own tediousness. The people wanted
theater."
Heinrich Mann
(quoted in *The Brothers Mann* by Nigel Hamilton)

"You'd be surprised how much being a good actor pays off."
Ronald Reagan
May 1, 1984

"It was Murrow who said 'Some stories don't have two sides.' At
Auschwitz he was right. But the news isn't always Auschwitz.
(Actually, if you get down deep, maybe a lot of stories are
Auschwitz, but TV doesn't get down deep.)"
Peggy "1000 Points O'Light" Noonan
(speechwriter for Presidents Reagan and Bush,
in *What I Saw at the Revolution*)

ACT ONE

Prologue:
Evening Meal in a Windstorm

(The empty apartment, 1990: repeated slides of a huge crowd rallying in support of Hitler, everyone giving the fascist salute. With each slide the people in the crowd draw nearer, till finally fixing on a single figure, a woman who isn't saluting. ZILLAH enters with a suitcase in hand. She is carrying a large book: a photo history of the Third Reich. She shows its open pages to the audience.)

ZILLAH: Ich bin eine Berliner.
Oh well not really.
Ich nicht eine Berliner, ich bin actually
eine Long Islander.
Ich bin Zillah Katz, nach Great Neck.
And that's all the German I know.

I don't know about you but for me,
the way I remember is usually in fact
a way of forgetting. Memory easily
becomes memorial: a blank stone marker
denoting: Event—
A tombstone under which
the bodies are buried, out of sight,
under which
the warning voice of what happened
is silenced.
Time now to remember, to recall: dismantle the memorial, disinter
the dead.

To call into the Now
other people, not my own;
an other city, not my own, an other people, not mine.
History. As I conjure it.

From out of too many nights spent
reading and dreaming,
from out of a book,
from out of a crowd: I find
one lonely
familiar
other face....
Now.

Slide: JANUARY 1, 1932.

(Lights up on AGNES' *apartment in Berlin. Seated around a table:* AGNES,
HUSZ, BAZ, PAULINKA *and* GOTCHLING. *It's night; the scene is lit by
candlelight. Everyone has been drinking.)*

GOTCHLING: Capitalism is a system of...of....

PAULINKA: Digestion! A digestive system!

HUSZ: We've drunk too much.

GOTCHLING: Again.

BAZ: I think I'm going to vomit....

PAULINKA: Ah! The advantages of opium.

AGNES: Midnight. HAPPY NEW YEAR!

(General exultation, "Happy New Year!")

AGNES: Oh... *(Laughs)*

GOTCHLING: What?

AGNES: Oh my... *(Laughs)*

BAZ: What? What?

AGNES: All of you. Look at your faces. It's a kind of perfect thing,
like a circle, a round perfection.

GOTCHLING: Well not so perfect. Time for coffee.

AGNES: No! I feel...what? Baz, what do I feel, I feel....

BAZ: Do you feel warm, Agnes?

AGNES: Yes.

BAZ: And...complete, Agnes?

AGNES: Complete? Mostly.

BAZ: Safe?

AGNES: Well...

BAZ: Relatively safe?

AGNES: We live in Berlin. It's 1932. I feel relatively safe.

HUSZ: Sufficient for the times. *(He stands up.)* Now I would like to propose a toast.

GOTCHLING: Excellent ideas! A man of ideas! Propose, Husz.

HUSZ: To Agnes!

GOTCHLING: To Agnes! Good-hearted and brave!

HUSZ: Occupant prima of our affections, immovable tenant of this small, solid room: health, happiness, and relative safety on this fierce and splendid night and for many years to come, dear heart.

EVERYONE: To Agnes.

(Silence)

PAULINKA: And in the silence, an angel passed over.

BAZ: Now what to do to begin the new year properly?

GOTCHLING: You were going to vomit.

BAZ: Yes, but now I have a better idea. Let's make up a story.

HUSZ: What kind of story?

BAZ: One we compose together. A story about...something.

GOTCHLING: About a cold night.

PAULINKA: A story about a cold night. Good. I begin.

BAZ: Please! This is Agnes' party. Agnes' apartment. Agnes should begin. Begin, Agnes.

AGNES: Oh, let's see....
   Ha! There was a winter once in Berlin when a terrible wind, cold as death, chased people through the streets at night and blew ice into their bones and killed them. Well, there was one man who had to walk to work late every evening....

GOTCHLING: He was a night watchman. And he said to himself, "This wind is murder." And he decided to spend his last hard-earned penny on a thick woolen coat and an extra-long scarf and then the night wind could blow all it liked, he'd be warm and safe. "Our humanity," he said to himself, "is defined through our struggle to overcome nature." So he did buy those things, and....

PAULINKA: And he wore them at night on his way to work, and the wind saw what he was up to, and it grew very angry and sharp, and it blew all the harder, and in seconds flat the man felt so cold he might as well have been naked. Score one for nature.

GOTCHLING: One for nature.

BAZ: And he knew his plan had failed, and the wind was killing him, so with blue and frozen lips he prayed to God to save him from the wind, but of course God didn't, and he caught a severe influenza.

HUSZ: And as he lay on his deathbed, he thought he heard the wind whistle, "Just you wait." His new coat and scarf hung from a peg on the wall. He could feel his life slipping away. He said to himself, "I wonder what's next?" and as he died he could hear the wind calling....

(GOTCHLING *blows out the candles.*)

AGNES: "Just you wait."

(*In the darkness, everyone laughs.*)

(*End of scene*)

Slide: JANUARY-JUNE 1932.
Slide: POLITICAL TENSION.
Slide: FIERCE FIGHTING, SOMETIMES IN THE STREET.
Slide: CRISIS / TRANSITIONAL PERIOD / CHANGE.
Slide: THE ISSUES ARE PARLIAMENTARY & REVOLUTIONARY.
Slide: THE WEIMAR COALITION IS A SHAKY AFFAIR.
Slide: AN UNEASY MARRIAGE OF LEFT-LIBERALS AND
    MODERATES.
Slide: IN APRIL, PRESIDENTIAL ELECTION.
Slide: HINDENBURG DEFEATS HITLER.
Slide: JANUARY-JUNE, 1932.

Scene One:
Love Scene with Lemon

Slide: MAY 30, 1932.

(AGNES listening to the radio: jazz. HUSZ enters.)

AGNES: Let's have sex.

HUSZ: Wait. A surprise.

AGNES: What?

(He pulls a lemon from his pocket, hands it to her.)

AGNES: Oh, a lemon! God, I haven't had a lemon in months!
You shouldn't have, Husz, they're so expensive....

HUSZ: Courtesy of the studio. I stole it from the set. I pretended
to be fiddling with the fruitbowl arrangement and.... *(Demonstrates
pocketing the lemon)*

AGNES: Let's have sex.

HUSZ: Not tonight.

AGNES: But I'm anxious tonight and I need to.

HUSZ: But I'm anxious too and I don't want to.

AGNES: Can I have a kiss?

HUSZ: Of course.

(They kiss.)

AGNES: I got a film.

HUSZ: How much?

AGNES: The rent at least. It's going to be a miserable film, swanboats
and parasols. I play a wise old lady in waiting for the Kaiserin. Lots
of jolly twinkles.

HUSZ: Germans should never try to be jolly. Present company
excepted, I hate all Germans.

AGNES: Marx was a German.

HUSZ: Marx was a Jew. With a London address. And the soul of a
Hungarian. I should never have left Hungary.

AGNES: They threw you out. You had to.

HUSZ: I should never have left Russia.

AGNES: If you wanted to stay in Russia you shouldn't have read Trotsky.

HUSZ: Read Trotsky, hell. I knew Trotsky. Goddamned Trotsky. In Russia we were making great films.

AGNES: But if you'd stayed there you'd never have met me, and my sensual compensations for artistic mediocrity.... Just a quick...?

HUSZ: I'm too anxious.

AGNES: Thanks for the lemon.

HUSZ: Small pleasures in bad times.

(End of scene)

Scene Two:
All Day in the Rain

Slide: MAY 30, 1932.

(Lights up on AGNES and PAULINKA.)

PAULINKA: His name is Dr. Bloom. He's a Jew with a big belly and bushy eyebrows. He has a red leather couch and a little picture of Freud framed in gold. I lie back and pretend I'm in Vienna.

AGNES: Sounds romantic.

PAULINKA: Romantic? It's unspeakably erotic. He has hair, dark hair, on the back of his hands. On his knuckles, like a wolf!

AGNES: What does he say about the opium?

PAULINKA: He doesn't know about that yet.

AGNES: I thought that was the point, the opium.

PAULINKA: No, not the point, this is psychoanalysis, there is no point, nothing so vulgar as that. The opium's mine. None of his business, really. Or yours.

AGNES: Then why bother?

PAULINKA: Because I am unhappy. Because I have to do something with all this money they pay me. Psychoanalysis makes more sense than communism. At least I don't have to pretend to read thick books with greasy pages and tiny print. At least I don't have to call dreadful sweaty people I don't like "comrade".

AGNES: It's important.

PAULINKA: It's dreary.

AGNES: Not some private little...

PAULINKA: I mean I have some reason to be on a couch. I have an ego. I have a superego. I have an id—maybe two or three. You don't have a political bone in your body.

AGNES: I do so. Apparently. Apparently I do.

PAULINKA: You didn't used to.

AGNES: I've changed.

PAULINKA: You aren't a communist.

AGNES: Not yet, but.
   I was walking to the studio, you know, past that office they have, the storefront on Leopold Street, and I stopped and I looked in the window, you know, the posters, the red flags, and I felt my lungs go all tight and I thought, well.... And I walked in and said, Hello I'm Agnes Eggling and I want to join the Party.

PAULINKA: Just like that. Bang.

AGNES: Well I've been thinking of doing it for a couple of months but basically bang, yes. Of course you can't just join up but they seemed very interested. I told them I was an actress and they asked me to do a skit.

PAULINKA: You'll make a fool of yourself.

AGNES: For the Transport Workers Strike Rally. Well not for the main rally but for sort of a...side rally.

PAULINKA: People throw things at strike rallies. This is a phase. You'll recover. Even I was a communist once.

AGNES: Impossible.

PAULINKA: Oh yes, full party membership. It lasted about two weeks. The communists make the best films, so I thought I'd sign up and then after the revolution I'd get all the good parts.

AGNES: And what if the Nazis made the best films?

PAULINKA: The Nazis? Their films are all about mountain-climbing.

AGNES: But if they did.

(PAULINKA *gives the Hitler salute.*)

AGNES: Pig.

PAULINKA: Pig yourself.

AGNES: Paulinka.

PAULINKA: Oh I know. I disappoint you. Well I disappoint myself. I do. But what can I do, I do what I can. Nothing compared to the Martyrdom of Red Agnes, Thespian for the Revolution, but....

AGNES: Last night I went to a big meeting. A man was giving a speech. I don't know who he was but he said things. That here is where capitalism will take its final stand. Here, in Germany. Not in twenty years, or forty, but soon. Today. If we go red the whole world will follow us. Everything bad and dangerous swept away.

PAULINKA: Imagine that.

AGNES: How can I stand back from that, Paulinka?

PAULINKA: I can't imagine.

AGNES: Paulinka, these are the most exciting days of my life.

(End of scene)

First Interruption:
Berlin 1990: Hysteria

(ZILLAH *and* ROLAND *are in the apartment.* ZILLAH *talks mostly to the audience, occasionally or when indicated to* ROLAND, *who listens to her with uncomprehending, friendly fascination.*)

ZILLAH: Berlin. When I told my parents I was leaving New York and moving to Berlin they reacted pretty much like I thought they would. *(She screams, she sobs.)* So why did I tell them? Because I always tell them everything I do. Because I am Basically Bourgeois. Take sleep, for instance: Sleep is essentially a bourgeois convention, right? I mean, no one who's looking open-eyed at all the awfulness there is everywhere would want to or in fact be able to sleep, any decent person should be too busy being hysterical to sleep, and when I was struck by the full realization of this, of what sleep really is, which happened at about 3:27AM Election Night 1980, I decided to break the chains of my middle-class epistemological predispositions, break the chains of Reason and Common Sense, and not sleep anymore, but because I am not a true hysteric, but rather a hysterical rationalist—which is not the same thing, it's a sort of self-cancelling term—I knew that my insomnia jag, going on its tenth year now thank you very much, would need a pharmaceutical boost to supplement the adrenalin rush I couldn't come by honestly through hysterical terror and I figured: I live in the East Village: Speed. Right? But I took No-Doz instead and why? Because Speed is drugs and it would upset my mother. Basically Bourgeois. I read too much for one thing, I mean people who have attained a really appropriate level of Panic in the face of for instance the 900th re-election of Jesse Helms—these true hysterics don't read much I imagine because, well, they can't sit still for that long—I read. This suitcase? No clothes: books. I am not a camera; I would like to be a camera; or maybe something more I don't know participatory than a camera even but instead I am the Zombie Graduate Student of the Living Dead. Except that I am nowhere matriculated. At large. In Berlin. *(To* ROLAND*)* Lenny Bernsteen—stein, was just in town conducting The Ninth, did you catch it, over by the Wall? Beethoven? Sprechen sie Beethoven?

ROLAND: Beethoven, ja. Er ist in der Stadt geboren, in der Ich geboren wurde.

ZILLAH: It was a big celebration in honor of the End of History and the end of Ideology and Re-Unification and all that, and Lenny did the Ninth only they changed the words of the Chorus: not freude anymore—freiheit.

ROLAND: Freiheit. Super.

ZILLAH: My German sucks but I read *Time* magazine: not joy. Freedom. Me, I would rather have freude. Freiheit's just another word for nothing left to lose. Lenny Lenny Lenny, oh what is the world coming to? Is this the end of history? And what am I doing here? In Berlin!

ROLAND: Ich denke, Beethoven ist da geboren. Jedenfalls, Ich bin es. Weißt du wo Leipzig ist?

ZILLAH: What?

ROLAND: Ich bin total doof. Ich habe nie Englisch lernen konnen. Französisch auch nicht.

ZILLAH: I'm sorry I don't.... We have a communications problem.

(End of scene)

Scene Three:
Late Night Struggles on Towards Dawn

Slide: May 30, 1932. LATE NIGHT.

(AGNES is alone, working on the skit. She has pencil, paper, various materials including The Red Baby— a doll— and a little Hitler doll.)

AGNES: *(Writes, then reads out loud)* Red Workers! Red Berlin! Arise! The world is perched on the brink of doom! *(She scratches out "doom", then writes, then reads:)* The world is perched on the brink of a catastrophe! *(She scratches out "catastrophe", then writes, then reads:)* The world is perched on the brink of a choice. The brink of a choice? Stupid. Stupid. Perched on the brink of...shit. *(She goes to the radio, turns it on: jazz music. She goes back to the table, picks up the little Hitler doll.)* Hello. I'm Adolf Hitler. Thank you for inviting me here on this lovely May morning. I love jazz. I love the dance music of dark-skinned peoples. Jewish wedding music. I love that! Dance with me! *(The doll dances a bit.)* Vote for me! Kiss my ass! Watch me fly in my aeroplane! Look up! Here I am! *(AGNES makes propeller noises and flies the little doll about the room. Then she crashes it with great relish.)* RED WORKERS! RED BERLIN! ARISE! THE WORLD IS PERCHED ON THE BRINK OF...SOMETHING...CHOOSE! COMMUNISM OR FASCISM! THE REVOLUTION OR DEATH! STRIKE! NOW! REVOLUTION! NOW!

HUSZ: *(From off in the bedroom)* Who are you screaming at?

AGNES: I'm working on the skit.

HUSZ: Work more quietly. I'm trying to sleep.

AGNES: Husz, what are we perched on the brink of?

HUSZ: Come to bed.

AGNES: Perched on the brink of...

HUSZ: Fascism. Old age. Senility. Sleep. *(He goes back to the bedroom, slams the door.)*

AGNES: *(Returning to the table)* Thanks. *(She picks up the lemon, cuts it open, sucks on it.)* Mmmm. Sour fruit. *(End of scene)*

Scene Three A:
Die Alte (The Old One)

Slide: MAY 30, 1932. AN HOUR AFTER MIDNIGHT.

(The apartment is very dark. AGNES is asleep at the table. DIE ALTE opens the window from without, and comes into the apartment. She sits opposite AGNES.)

DIE ALTE: I remember the day: a sky
so bright that beneath it
every thought is drowned, save
innocence. Summer
but the sun's a chill apricot light,
high up,
a dense, brilliant haze— an immense
day...
War was declared.
Which war, I don't remember.
We wore corsets then;
rigid, with the tusks of whales;
they pinched, and often
bruises and blood. But
that was a wonderful time.
I heard the snap of the flags
crack in the wind, and the men marched past.
Something hot moved through me that day,
up through the ribs of the corset—
it was my heart. I remember that.
A wonderful time, not
now...
Now. Hungry. Always. Never
enough.

(AGNES *stirs in her sleep.*)

DIE ALTE: *(With quiet fear)* Ahhh...

(*End of scene*)

Scene Four:
Cold and Brutal but Exact and True

Slide: JUNE 2, 1932.

(AGNES *is alone with a glass of wine, struggling with the opening pages of* Kapital. BAZ *enters without knocking, followed by* GOTCHLING.)

BAZ: Guess where we've been.

AGNES: Where?

GOTCHLING: At a Nazi rally.

(BAZ *produces a swastika pennant which he waves about.*)

AGNES: You went inside?

BAZ: You must have an intimate knowledge of the enemy.

GOTCHLING: He thought I should see it happening first hand.

AGNES: See what happening?

BAZ: The floodgates breaking open. The sewers backing up. Gotchling saw some old friends there.

GOTCHLING: A year ago I designed a series of posters for the Party office in Wedding. Tonight I recognized at least ten "comrades" from the district. Devout communists. Now they're wearing swastikas.

BAZ: Right. Like bugs to a gaslamp. The Nazis make more noise, so bzzzzz. They attract the most insects. Fine specimens of Germanity, looking high and low—well, low, mostly, for any release for their desperately trapped sexual energies.

GOTCHLING: Oh not this crap again...

BAZ: Well they won't find it in the Communist Party. Membership requires a doctorate in hypocrisy. Let's see, which leg are we going to stand on this week, the left or the right? Can't decide? Call Stalin!

GOTCHLING: Ah, political clarity from the Institute of Human Depravity.

BAZ: Sexuality! Human Sexuality.

GOTCHLING: You know, dear, just because they employ you doesn't mean you have to listen to their ridiculous theories. If sexual frustration was the cause, everyone would be a fascist.

BAZ: Glib reductionist.

GOTCHLING: Sex maniac. When Hitler reveals himself as just another flunky for German capital, the working class will abandon him.

AGNES: They'll destroy him.

GOTCHLING: Absolutely!

BAZ: Economic analysis! So antiseptic! So sterile! The fascists don't try to make sense. They abandon morality, money, justice—Hitler simply offers a lot of very confused and terrified and constipated people precisely what they want, a means of release. These people are far beyond caring whether Hitler is a socialist or not. They're in love with the shine on his boots, they want a fatherly bootheel to lick, they want him to say "Daddy loves his children, now go and kill for me." They're completely deaf to your hairsplitting pseudoscience and jolly-comrade goodwill. They want bloody things.

GOTCHLING: Baz, you're a slob, an intellectual slob.

BAZ: Ouch. And I thought I was penetrating to the very heart of the Mystery of the Decade.

GOTCHLING: You're never going to make a coherent political theory based on orgasms. These people are frightened because the capitalists can't tell them how to save themselves and they haven't heard us yet. They will. The preconditions for revolution are in the making.

BAZ: Do I detect a note of uncertainty?

GOTCHLING: No. I know people will make a lot of mistakes. A drowning man clutches at twigs.

BAZ: Yes. But this particular twig may very well save them.

AGNES: (Scoffing) Hitler? How!?

BAZ: Once he's chancellor he'll build an army and start looking for a war. Guns make jobs, right, comrade? It won't be hard convincing

Hindenburg or the German people. Germans love guns, more than jobs. And before...

AGNES: *(Sounding a little spoon-fed and undigested)* Not true! The system can't recover from the Crash!

BAZ: Says who?

AGNES: Everyone. It hasn't yet. Its decline is Historically Inevitable. And for another thing, the German proletariat doesn't want war.

BAZ: I submit, Agnes, that you are a middle-class actress who knows very little about the German proletariat.

AGNES: I know enough. And I submit, Baz, that you are a condescending snob whose homosexuality alienates him from the proletariat.

BAZ: Indeed? *(To* GOTCHLING*)* Is she learning this from you?

AGNES: And your theories, by the way, of sexual repression as the root of all evil are half-baked.

BAZ: Half-baked. This from a Marxist who's never read Marx!

AGNES: I have so!

BAZ: *The Communist Manifesto* doesn't count. Everyone's read that! And my being homosexual brings me into contact with more proletarians than you can imagine.

AGNES: So does working at the studio.

BAZ: Right. They paint your face and clean up after you've finished acting. I have sex with them.

GOTCHLING: And they tell you they're voting for Hitler?

BAZ: Some do.

GOTCHLING: Do you still sleep with them?

BAZ: I'll never tell.

AGNES: Baz!

BAZ: What?

AGNES: You'd sleep with a Nazi?

BAZ: I didn't say that. You sleep with a Trotskyite.

AGNES: That's different.

BAZ: Not to Stalin it isn't.

AGNES: Evasion.

BAZ: I have to get to work.

AGNES: More evasion.

BAZ: No but I do. The Institute is doing a big poster campaign.
Abortion on demand. Free condoms. Great big posters. The Nazis
will adore them. In the face of an erupting volcano we struggle
hopelessly, hopelessly....

AGNES: Not hopelessly.

BAZ: Who can say? Prophecy is sorcery, sorcery is a sin.

GOTCHLING: More slop. It'll be money in the end, you wait—capital
for the fascists and the workers for themselves. Bad time to be
wasting time. Join the Party.

BAZ: I can't.

GOTCHLING: Why not?

BAZ: They won't let me wear mascara. Good night. *(He exits.)*

AGNES: *(To* GOTCHLING*)* Do you think he sleeps with Nazis?

(End of scene)

Slide: July 21-November 6, 1932.
Slide: IN JULY, PARLIAMENTARY ELECTIONS.
Slide: THE NAZIS WIN 37% OF THE POPULAR VOTE.
Slide: THIS IS THE LARGEST GENUINE VOTE THEY WILL
    EVER RECEIVE.
Slide: THEY NOW WIELD A PARLIAMENTARY MAJORITY.
Slide: THE COALITION OF LIBERAL-CENTER PARTIES,
Slide: THE "WEIMAR COALITION",
Slide: HAS BEEN DEFEATED.
Slide: THEN, IN NOVEMBER, MORE PARLIAMENTARY
    ELECTIONS.
Slide: COMMUNISTS GAIN 12 SEATS, THE NAZIS LOSE 34.
Slide: A SHARP REVERSAL IN FASCIST POPULARITY IS WIDELY
    PREDICTED.

Slide: BUT THE NAZIS STILL CONTROL A PARLIAMENTARY MAJORITY.

Scene Five:
Fingerspitzengefühl (Fingertip Feeling)

Slide: JULY 21, 1932. NATIONAL REICHSTAG ELECTIONS.

(AGNES *and* PAULINKA *sit over toast and coffee at the table.*)

PAULINKA: She met him at a fancy dress dinner a year ago. Nazis and tycoons. She was this close, and she swears to me that his little black moustache is not made of hair.

AGNES: What's it made of?

PAULINKA: She couldn't tell. Something hard and shiny. Beetle wings, who knows.

AGNES: That's ridiculous.

PAULINKA: You hear all sorts if things. You know that in Munich he developed an incestuous infatuation for his cousin. He forced her to live with him and a whole lot more besides. She killed herself. She was seventeen. And at the studio I heard from someone who has a brother high up in the Party that every woman who winds up in his bed either kills herself or has an accident or is found murdered later.

AGNES: Oh that's nonsense.

PAULINKA: You don't believe it? I do.

AGNES: Who wants to know about his perversions?

PAULINKA: They say he's a coprophilic.

AGNES: A what?

PAULINKA: Shit.

AGNES: OH PAULINKA, PLEASE, THAT'S DISGUSTING!

PAULINKA: I didn't make it up. This woman told me that she actually knows a high-priced prostitute who spent the night with him. She won't talk about what happened or what's got her so scared, but now she's in terror for her life. She rarely leaves her flat these days and she always feels cold.

AGNES: I don't want to hear anymore.

PAULINKA: Agnes, do you believe in evil?

AGNES: It's not something you believe in. There are evil men, of course.

PAULINKA: Diabolical evil?

AGNES: What are you asking me?

PAULINKA: Do you believe in the Devil, Agnes? That's what I'm asking you. Do you believe in the Devil?

AGNES: At my age?

PAULINKA: Because I do.

Scene Five A:
It Takes Three Invitations

(There is a sudden change of lighting: the room grows dim, and a brilliant spotlight hits PAULINKA, *who warms to it immediately and begins to address the audience.)*

PAULINKA: I've seen Him. Well, not Him, exactly, or... When I had just started acting I did two seasons at the Municipal Theater of Karlsruhe. Ever been to Karlsruhe? *(She smiles; it is a telling smile.)* We were giving Faust, Part One, a play I've always detested, and I was playing Gretchen, a part I've always detested, and I was not happy, not happy at all. There were nights I thought I'd be stuck in the provinces forever, never see Berlin, never see the inside of a film studio, die, go to hell, and it'd be exactly like Karlsruhe. Black nights, you could imagine your whole life gone.... You know the scene in the play where the black poodle turns into the devil and offers Faust the world? All that demurring, endless, always seemed so coy to me. Just... But, so, one night I was walking home after a performance and a very strange thing happened. I found myself going down a narrow street, an alley, really, one I'd never been down before, and suddenly.... There was this little black poodle, sitting on a doorstep. Waiting for me. Staring at me with those wet dark dog eyes. And I thought to myself: "It's Him! He's come to talk to me!" He's going to stand up on His little hind-legs and say "Paulinka! Fame, films, and unsurpassable genius as an actor in exchange for your immortal soul!" And that's when I knew it, and my dears I wish I didn't know: I'd never resist. I couldn't. I am constitutionally incapable of resisting anything. A good actress, a good liar, but not in truth a very good person. Just give me Berlin, sixty years of success, and then haul me off to the Lake of Fire! Do business with the Devil. But so anyway the poodle had other things in mind. I guess I must have startled it when I asked it if it wanted to make me an offer. It leaped up at me, barking and snarling and obviously out for blood. Chased me for blocks. I escaped by ducking into a bar, where I drank and drank and drank.... Probably just somebody's nasty black poodle. But I've always wondered...what if it really was Him, and He decided I wasn't worth it? *(End of scene)*

Scene Six:
Demonology

Slide: SEPTEMBER 12, 1932.

(AGNES alone, sitting with Kapital, *flipping the pages distractedly. There is a loud knock. She goes to answer it.)*

MALEK: *(Entering)* Comrade Eggling, we come as specially designated representatives of the Party's Central Committee. We've been sent to convey congratulations to you and your comrade collaborators for a highly successful agitprop performance.

AGNES: Oh well thank you that's very....

TRAUM: *(Entering behind* MALEK*)* Long live the Revolution! Long live Germany!

AGNES: YES! Yes. Can I get you some...tea or....

MALEK: We hope you'll continue to contribute your efforts to the struggle.

AGNES: Oh absolutely. I mean, I intend to. I don't usually, but...well, as much as I can. Absolutely, I...

TRAUM: Good. One other matter. There are certain Left-deviationist tendencies in your play that must be corrected before it can be performed again. Which hopefully will be very soon.

AGNES: Left-deviationist tendencies?

MALEK: Small problems, really.

TRAUM: Well, not so small...

MALEK: Fairly small.

TRAUM: Actually fairly large.

MALEK: Fairly small. *(Tiny uneasy pause. To* AGNES:*)* It would be more appropriate, in keeping with current Party policy....

TRAUM: *(Consulting a notebook)* Look. This is the play about the Red Baby?

AGNES: Right. The Red Baby Play.

TRAUM: Highly amusing. The Red Baby... What is the Red Baby, Comrade?

AGNES: It's...well, it's a symbol...a symbol of...of....

MALEK: Of the newborn proletarian revolution.

AGNES: Exactly.

TRAUM: Exactly.

AGNES: What?

TRAUM: Exactly. Exactly the problem. Look, Comrade, as you probably already know the most recent directives of the Comintern Executive have....

MALEK: Comrade Eggling, the focus of your play is very clearly the proletarian revolution in Germany, that it's going to happen very soon.

AGNES: Yes.

MALEK:	TRAUM:
Well the difficulty is....	Exactly. And that is no longer an accurate reflection of the policy of the Comintern, nor of the KPD.

AGNES: It isn't?

TRAUM: No. It is Left-deviationist adventurist opportunism.

*(*AGNES *doesn't get it.)*

TRAUM: You're rushing things.

AGNES: You mean there isn't going to be a proletarian revolution?

MALEK:	TRAUM:
Well of course there has been one	Oh, well,

in Russia. In Germany...   eventually, yes,
eventually, yes, but it's not   but...
the next step.

AGNES: What's the next step?

TRAUM: Defense of Soviet Russia.

AGNES: But in Germany? Here?

MALEK: Well, a United Front against Fascism...

TRAUM: But not with the Social Democrats.

MALEK: No. No. Not with the Social Democrats.

(Again a tiny, uneasy pause)

MALEK: TRAUM:
Well what we mean by that is....   Well, with the Social Democrat
                                         workers but not the leaders.
                                         The SPD leadership must be
                                         exposed as Social Fascist and
                                         hence indistinguishable from
                                         the Nazis.

MALEK: Well, not indistinguishable.

TRAUM: Oh yes.

MALEK: No.

TRAUM: Yes! The Comintern's position on this....

MALEK: You're wrong! Not even the Comintern is stupid enough to
say that.

TRAUM: Oh yes they are!

MALEK: You're wrong, Comrade.

TRAUM: *(Pulling rank)* NO! YOU are!

(There is a very uneasy pause.)

TRAUM: We feel certain that in time the workers loyal to the SPD will
come over to us.

AGNES: It looks like more of them are going over to the Nazis.

MALEK: True.

TRAUM: No! Not true! I mean it looks that way but....

AGNES: If there's not going to be a United Front with the Social Democrats then who are you going to be united with?

TRAUM: Look. It's not our fault. They don't want us either.

AGNES: Maybe you should stop calling them fascists.

TRAUM: But they are fascists.

AGNES: No they're not.

TRAUM: Yes they are.

MALEK: No they're not!

TRAUM: MALEK!

MALEK: Well you know them same as I do. They aren't.

TRAUM: As Comrade Malek knows perfectly well, holding a firm line against bourgeois parliamentary dictatorships is essential to the revolution.

AGNES: But there isn't going to be a revolution!

MALEK: Oh yes there is!

AGNES: He said there wasn't.

MALEK: Well, he's wrong.

TRAUM: NO, YOU ARE!

MALEK: NO, YOU ARE!

(Silence)

AGNES: Just tell me what to do with the Red Baby.

MALEK: We're not artists, Comrade. You work it out. Try to de-emphasize the importance—the immediate importance—of revolution. The workers aren't ready yet.

AGNES: (To MALEK) Do you believe this, Comrade....

MALEK: Malek. Rosa Malek. No. But I believe in Party discipline.

TRAUM: I noticed.
   We would also suggest that the Red Baby not be identified as proletarian. We're trying to sell the new concept of the KPD as a

party for everyone, not just the workers. "Class struggle" seems to scare the petty-bourgeois right into the arms of the Nazis.

AGNES: I'll do what I can.

MALEK: Thank you, Comrade. We appreciate it.

TRAUM: It's extremely important.

AGNES: It's just a skit.

TRAUM: No. Every effort from every corner brings us closer to victory.

(Tiny uncomfortable pause. TRAUM leaves.)

MALEK: You know, Comrade, your play gave me nightmares.

AGNES: It did?

MALEK: The Red Baby. I don't mean this as a criticism but it's awful when you think about it, a red baby. Imagine a real red baby. Wouldn't that be horrible, like someone had painted it or boiled it or something.

AGNES: Horrible.

MALEK: I don't remember the dream, what happened. But it was a nightmare because I woke up all tangled in the sheets.

(MALEK gives AGNES the KPD salute. AGNES returns it. They stare at each other. MALEK exits.)

(End of scene)

Scene Seven:
Scenes from the Life: First Part

Slide: NOVEMBER 6, 1932. SECOND NATIONAL REICHSTAG ELECTIONS.

(AGNES is listening to the radio for election news. GOTCHLING enters with her portfolio.)

AGNES: Twelve new seats! We got twelve!

GOTCHLING: I know.

AGNES: And they lost thirty-four! Thirty-four fascists out the door! Millions of votes! They're losing!

GOTCHLING: *(Taking materials out of portfolio)* Help with...

AGNES: WE WON! We're going to win! Up and up! And I feel like I helped, like I actually moved in time, the lump moved!

GOTCHLING: Cut this along the blackened edges. And be careful.

AGNES: Gotchling! You MUST be happy tonight! Even you!

(Small pause)

GOTCHLING: My father had a little speech, we'd get it every night after he'd read the papers. "People are pigs" he'd say. "Human history isn't the story of the good man, not of the saint, but of the swine who bludgeoned the saint to death. Fond of mud, full of shit, pigs. In my many years on earth, this is what I've learned." Every night while he ate his onions, word for word. He couldn't let go of it—that contempt or despair or whatever the hell it was. "People are pigs." And last week when I thought the Nazis were going to add thirty-four seats I found myself saying "people are pigs", like a chant. But then they surprise you. The People. Five million come out of their rooms and they vote communist. Which is not easy for them to do. Five million people.

(HUSZ enters without knocking.)

GOTCHLING: *(Suddenly, at the top of her lungs)* FIVE MILLION PEOPLE, HUSZ!

(HUSZ pulls two enormous bottles of vodka from inside his coat.)

HUSZ: Tonight, we swallow our differences. Fire, Annabella. In the street, in our throats, in the sky. Red fire. The ground is shaking.

GOTCHLING: FIRE!

HUSZ: I have felt this before. The masses are on the move.

(End of scene)

Scene Seven A:
Scenes from the Life: Second Part

Slide: NOVEMBER 6, 1932. LATER THE SAME NIGHT.

(HUSZ, AGNES, and GOTCHLING, who is working on a collage, cutting and pasting. No one is drunk, but everyone's been drinking.)

HUSZ: Scenes from the life of Vealtninc Husz, one-eyed cameraman: Russian Episodes. One: I make Trotsky weep. Interior shot, overhead pan of huge crowd milling, the Red Artists Congress in Leningrad, 1921. *(He hums the opening notes of the* Internationale, *then:)* Dolly in to big knot of people surrounding Comrade Trotsky, mingling; track along behind him till he reaches the great Dziga-Vertov. Close up on handshake: the marriage of politics and art. Trotsky notices among DV's entourage a young Hungarian with an eye patch, asks Dziga-Vertov, "The Hungarian, what happened to his eye?" Dziga-Vertov replies, "His name is Husz, he lost it in the revolution in Budapest, Comrade Trotsky." Close up on Husz, his black eye patch; jump to close-up of eye of Trotsky, behind its thick, magnifying lens. Looking at Husz. Trotsky: with a big wet tear in his eye. *(Pause; he gets another drink.)* Music!

GOTCHLING: *(Singing)* Arise, ye prisoners of starvation,
Arise, ye wretched of the earth.
For justice thunders condemnation,
A better world's in birth.

HUSZ: Two. Huge close-up, the mouth of Dziga-Vertov, thin-lipped, saying "Film is the perfect medium, the only medium for the age of machines, because it is mechanically made, not focused on the small inner life but on the grand scale, capable of recording an entire revolution!" Jump to the ear of Husz, deep, empty, listening, filling up. Interior shot, from the ear to the heart. In German film studios, nobody listens. Music!

GOTCHLING: *(Singing)* No more, tradition's chains shall bind us,
Arise ye poor, no more in thrall.
The earth shall rise on new foundations,
We have been naught, we shall be all!

HUSZ: Three: Dream sequence, like from Hollywood.

(GOTCHLING *starts whistling a high-pitched, dreamy* Internationale *chorus.)*

HUSZ: Map of Europe, borders drawn in black, heavy lines.
Flames eat it up, revealing
carved in granite, the lovely word
"Internationalism."
Cross-fade to a magnificent expanse,
a valley,

mountains,
and millions of people, simply millions,
so many that the valley is completely filled,
each an infinitely precious part of a glorious entirety—
Comrades, together, calling Paradise
home.

(HUSZ *sings, then* GOTCHLING, *and then* AGNES, *join in.*)

ALL THREE: *(Singing)* 'Tis the final conflict;
Let each stand in their place;
The Internationale
Unites the human race.
'Tis the final conflict;
Let each stand in their place;
The Internationale
Will be the human race!

HUSZ: End of film.

(End of scene)

Slide: NOVEMBER 6-JANUARY 1, 1932.
Slide: STAGNATION AND SINKING.
Slide: THE LEFT'S EARLY VICTORIES ARE NOT EXPANDED
   UPON.
Slide: THE CATHOLIC CENTER SHIFTS ALLIANCES
Slide: TOWARDS THE FASCIST RIGHT.
Slide: BIG-MONEY SUPPORT FOR A HITLER CHANCELLORSHIP.
Slide: A DIM AND OPPRESSIVE AWARENESS AMONG THE
   PEOPLE
Slide: THAT THE BATTLE HAS TURNED
Slide: AWAY FROM THE STREETS AND THE BALLOT BOX
Slide: TO SECRET DEALS BETWEEN POWERFUL PEOPLE
Slide: IN PRIVATE ROOMS.

Scene Eight:
Ich habe eine neue Giftsuppe gekocht
(I Made a New Poison Soup)

Slide: NOVEMBER 6, 1932. EVEN LATER.

(The room is dark; DIE ALTE is at the table again, grinding. AGNES enters from the bedroom, turns on the light. DIE ALTE looks up at AGNES, who is startled.)

AGNES: Oh!

DIE ALTE: Do you have something to eat?

(AGNES hesitates, staring, then moves to the cupboard and takes an apple from a bowl. She puts it on the table.)

DIE ALTE: Something softer? Cheese?

AGNES: Do you live here? In this building?

(Small pause. DIE ALTE looks at AGNES.)

DIE ALTE: There's an iron stairs outside the window.

AGNES: The fire escape?

DIE ALTE: Do you have something to eat? The price of things. It's unbearable.

AGNES: You came down the fire escape?

DIE ALTE: The wind's strong there. I press up against the bricks, they're cold, my gown whips against the railing, my cheeks burn. Bread if you don't have cheese.

(There is a loud metallic knock in the walls.)

AGNES: The water pipes.

DIE ALTE: Sounds like knocking. Little penny man. Let him in.

AGNES: *(Back to the cupboard)* I think I have some rolls.

DIE ALTE: Just before I fall asleep,
After God has heard my prayers,
Things below begin to creep:
The penny man is on the stairs.

AGNES: Oh, I remember that poem, years ago....

DIE ALTE: The rolls, please.

(AGNES gives her a roll. She begins to eat, greedily.)

DIE ALTE: It's a little stale.

(End of scene)

Second Interruption:
Berlin 1990: History

(ZILLAH *and* ROLAND. *Books everywhere.* ROLAND *is looking at the pictures.)*

ZILLAH: What did your daddy do in the War?

ROLAND: Vielleicht sollen wir 'was essen gehen. Indisch?

ZILLAH: I've always wanted to ask a German that. In New York I met plenty of Germans but they all spoke English so I never had the nerve; you I can ask and you won't be offended or guilty or anything because you won't understand the question and I don't understand the answer. It's perfect.

ROLAND: Ich bin noch jungfraulich. Außerdem, bin ich Sozialist, ich bin nicht nach dem Westen gefahren, um Tennisschuhe zu kaufen, aber ich würde schon gern mal bumsen.

ZILLAH: Wow. This city; this language: history, right? Even him, I have no idea who this guy is, I picked him up in some bar my first night here, I mean like don't you ever go home or anything? All right so he's a little young to be historical but still he looks like them, like they looked back then, in all those black-and-white photos they took of themselves.... Or this apartment—I knew when I got here I didn't want one of those economic miracle aluminum/linoleum events, I wanted this: a squat nineteenth-century job that made it through the bombings. It's tonic, all this historical grit. History: it smells like garbage. Wonderful.

ROLAND: Ich glaube, ich sollte dich warnen, ich bin vielleicht bisexuel. Ich fühle mich schwindlig.

ZILLAH: Me? Oh I just couldn't hack it back in the United States of Amnesia. The last decade was too hard for a history junkie like myself—The Decade of the Great Commmunicator. Your Great Communicator spoke and created a whole false history, ours spoke and history basically came down with arteriosclerosis; from the Triumph of the Will to the Triumph of the Brain-Dead—from National Socialism to National Senility. Eight years of watching him try to remember his lines; it was our national cliffhanger: Is he finally going to go totally blank in front of an audience of 3.6 billion people and just stand there waggling his head, you know the way he does—

(She does it.) "Shake up those neurons, something'll come."—
and this is a Great Communicator? YES! Because what he was
communicating to a nation that wanted desperately to go to sleep
and get lost in dreams because reality was becoming too damn ugly
was: "FORGET EVERYTHING, FOLKS." Because what Reagan
communicated is that you can be even more divorced from History
and Reality and Language than he was from Jane Wyman and STILL
BE THE MOST POWERFUL MAN ON EARTH!

ROLAND: Reagan?

ZILLAH: Reagan.

ROLAND: *(Doing Reagan with an nearly impenetrable German accent)*
"Mister Gorbachev, tear down this wall!" Ich hab 's im Fernsehen
gesehen.

ZILLAH: And after the twenty-five people who bothered to vote in
1988 voted for the Kennebunkport Katastrophe and the party that
bought you Iran-Contra, I said to myself nuts to this, I need to
reconnect with history, I need to find some ghosts, I need to go
someplace so haunted there's no way to hide the haunts—back to
the basics, I said to myself, back to the bone. Back, in point of fact,
to Berlin.

(End of scene)

Scene Nine:
Love Scene Without Lemon

Slide: DECEMBER 4, 1932.

*(AGNES alone, Kapital face down on table. Radio playing jazz. The music
stops and Hitler's voice comes on. AGNES switches the radio off. HUSZ
enters in a hurry.)*

HUSZ: Now let's have sex.

AGNES: Not now, I don't want to.

HUSZ: But I need to. I'm anxious tonight.

AGNES: I can't. I'm too anxious.

HUSZ: We have to get together on this.

AGNES: Kiss.

(They do.)

AGNES: Did you enjoy that?

HUSZ: Not particularly, no.

AGNES: They say he'll be chancellor. Hindenburg is very old.

HUSZ: *(Tired, with little conviction)* There'll be uprisings. His government will be short-lived.

AGNES: For a thousand years.

HUSZ: *(Laughs)* Nothing ever lasts that long.

AGNES: Lately I feel like I'm in a film, all the time. A newsreel. I see all these events already on film, not just Hitler, but us: no sex, eating and crying. All public events. There is a title: "PERCHED ON THE BRINK OF A GREAT HISTORIC CRIME".

HUSZ: Indeed.

AGNES: And you want to have sex? At a time like this?

HUSZ: I'm anxious.

(End of scene)

Scene Ten:
The Rent

Slide: JANUARY 1, 1933.

(AGNES alone. It's late at night. The apartment is dimly lit.)

AGNES: I can see myself living here
through a hurricane or fire—
even if the building was burning
I think I'd stay.
Why?
Do you know how hard it is
to find an apartment in Berlin?

(As AGNES continues to speak, beautiful, intense sunlight begins to stream through the windows.)

AGNES: I feel at home.
My friends like it here,
better than their own apartments.

I'm not a fool.
I know that what's coming
will be bad,
but not unliveable,
and not eternally,
and when it's over, I will have clung to the least last thing,
which is to say, my lease.
And you have to admit, it's a terrific apartment.
I could never find anything like it if I moved out now.
You would not believe
how low the rent is.

(*End of scene*)

Slide: JANUARY 30, 1933.
Slide: PRESIDENT HINDENBURG
Slide: APPOINTS ADOLF HITLER
Slide: CHANCELLOR OF THE GERMAN REICH.

Scene Eleven:
Oranges

(AGNES *and* BAZ. *Night.* BAZ *is kneeling on the floor, praying.*)

BAZ: I see no reason to be ashamed. In the face of genuine hopelessness one has no choice but to gracefully surrender reason to the angelic hosts of the irrational. They alone bring solace and comfort, for which we say, in times of distress, "Hosannah and who needs science?"

AGNES: But then you're saying it's all right to admit defeat.

BAZ: Well, when one is defeated....

AGNES: But see, that's just the problem. How do we know? What if we lay down and give up just at the moment when....

BAZ: When what?

AGNES: When the whole terrible thing could somehow have been reversed.

BAZ: Do you really think it can? The farmers say, "If we could grow wheat in the winter then we wouldn't be so hungry." But does that mean anything to the groundlock and the frost? No. So the farmers wait till spring. What we need is a Meteorology of Human History. Then maybe we could weather the changes in the political climate with as much composure as we weather changes in the weather. Seasons of History. Does it matter if we know why it rains? It just rains. We get wet. Or not. Life is miserable. Or not. The sun shines, or it doesn't shine. You can explain these things, scientifically, meteorologically, and we can applaud the elegance of your explanation, but it won't stop the weather, or that telling feeling of being overwhelmed. Because on this planet, one is overwhelmed.

AGNES: Gotchling would call that defeatist crap.

BAZ: Gotchling. Gotchling is out at this very moment nailing posters to telephone poles. But you and I...

AGNES: I remember once I was out all day in the rain, and the sky was dark from morning on, but just before night the rain stopped, and between the black sky and the ground there was a small open space, a thin band of day that stretched across the rim of the world. And as I watched, night came and the ground and sky closed shut. I'm overwhelmed. I feel no connection, no kinship with most of the people I see. I watch them in the underground come and go and I think, "Are you a murderer? Are you?" And there are so many people.

BAZ: Yesterday I was on my way to buy oranges. I eat them constantly in the winter, even though they cost so much, because they prevent colds. On my way to the grocer's I passed a crowd in front of an office building; I asked what was going on and they showed me that a man had jumped from the highest floor and was dead. They had covered the man with tar paper but his feet were sticking out at angles that told you something was very wrong. There was a pink pool of red blood mixed with white snow. I left. At the grocer's I felt guilty and embarrassed buying these fat oranges for myself only minutes after this man had died. I knew why he had jumped. I thought of him opening the window, high up, and the cold air.... On my way home I reimagined the whole thing, because I felt a little sick at heart. The dead man was sitting up in the snow, and now the tar paper covered his feet. As I passed by I gave him one of my oranges. He took it. He stared at the orange, as though holding it could give him back some of the warmth he'd lost. All day, when I closed my eyes, I could see him that way. Sitting in the snow, holding the orange, and comforted. Still bloody, still dead, but...comforted.

AGNES: I'm not very scientific. I really believed once that oranges prevented colds because they store up hot sunlight in the tropical places they grow and the heat gets released when you eat one.

BAZ: I consider that a perfectly scientific explanation, and probably correct.
    These are cold days, not to be believed.

(End of scene)

Scene Twelve:
Furcht und Elend (Fear and Misery)

Slide: JANUARY 30, 1933. LATER THAT NIGHT.

(AGNES, HUSZ, PAULINKA, GOTCHLING, *and* BAZ. *The wreckage of an unhappy evening lies scattered about.*)

GOTCHLING: The times are what we make them.

HUSZ: And we will make them unliveable.

BAZ: Touché.

GOTCHLING: Things may get tough for a bit.

HUSZ: A bit?

GOTCHLING: More than a bit.

HUSZ: A very long time. To be replaced by something that looks like progress but will turn out to be worse than what it replaced. *(He starts for the bedroom.)*

GOTCHLING: Where are you going?

HUSZ: To piss. Out the window. *(Exits)*

PAULINKA: I once said to Rollo Jaspers, "If you didn't fill your films with such hateful, stupid people the world wouldn't look so bad to you." And he said, "I fill my films with the kind of hateful, stupid people the world is full of. Look around you." And at that precise moment, everyone in the vicinity was remarkably hateful and stupid and I had to concede the point. Depressing memory.

GOTCHLING: Opium is the perfect drug for people who want to remain articulate while being completely trivial.

BAZ: I'm off. It's been a lovely wake. Happy eternity, give my best to the corpse.

GOTCHLING: You shouldn't go out.

BAZ: I know, but the teagardens, my dear. The night is calling.

GOTCHLING: They're celebrating.

BAZ: I want to celebrate too. The end of a very long and painful struggle. Never knew it'd be such a relief!

GOTCHLING: Sometimes...

BAZ: Yes?

(HUSZ *reenters from the bedroom.*)

GOTCHLING: (To BAZ, *very angry*) I could strike you.

(*Silence.* BAZ *goes to* GOTCHLING, *kisses her forehead, and exits.*)

GOTCHLING: All of you. This elegant despair. You pretend to be progressive but actually progress distresses you. It's untidy, upsetting. Fortunately it happens anyway.

HUSZ: So I believed. I journeyed to the home of progress. I gave it an eye. Progress ate it up, crunch crunch, and said, "You have two eyes, give me another!" And I said, "Oh no thanks, I'm leaving."

GOTCHLING: And so you left and turned into a reactionary.

HUSZ: No. I didn't. I can't become a reactionary because that eye, part of me, is to this day lying in the belly of Progress and it will never let me go. The eye I have left looks clearly at all the shit in front of it, but the eye I gave to the revolution will always see what it saw then....

GOTCHLING: That was the good eye. This one's diseased. Too much Trotsky!

HUSZ: The last true revolutionary, may God keep him! Everyone else has surrendered.

GOTCHLING: Morbid dry rot! I hate arguing with you, Husz. I used to enjoy it, but you've become a bitter old bore.

HUSZ: Sweet Annabella.

PAULINKA: We are such rotten people.

AGNES: No. Don't say that.

GOTCHLING: We may be. History will move on without us.

PAULINKA: We are frightened and faithless. What's inside is an unstable, decomposing mess. Everyone on the street, looking tidy, just thin-skinned vessels full of grey, reeking, swampy pulp....
(She starts to get nauseated.)

HUSZ: Listen!

(Everyone except PAULINKA *is immediately alert.* GOTCHLING *goes to the window.)*

HUSZ: Do you hear something?

GOTCHLING: No, I...

HUSZ: Listen, Paulinka...

PAULINKA: What? I don't....

HUSZ: Shut up. Listen.
There is something calling, Paulinka.
If you still retain a shred of decency
you can hear it—it's a dim terrible
voice that's calling—a bass howl, like
a cow in a slaughterhouse, but
far, far off....
It is calling us to action, calling us
to stand against the calamity,
to spare nothing, not our blood,
nor our happiness, nor our lives
in the struggle to stop the dreadful day
that's burning now
in oil flames on the horizon.

What makes the voice pathetic
is that it doesn't know
what kind of people it's reaching.
Us.
No one hears it, except us.
This age wanted heroes.

It got us instead: carefully constructed, but
immobile.
Subtle, but
unfit to take up
the burden of the times.
It happens: A whole generation of washouts.
History says stand up,
and we totter and collapse,
weeping, moved, but not
sufficient.

The best of us, lacking.
The most decent,
not decent enough.
The kindest,
too cruel,
the most loving
too full of hate,
the wisest,
too stupid,
the fittest
unfit
to take up
the burden of the times.

The enemy
has a voice like seven thunders.
What chance did that dim voice ever have?
Marvel that anyone heard it
instead of wondering why nobody did anything,
marvel that we heard it,
we who have no right to hear it—
NO RIGHT!
And it would be a mercy not to.
But mercy...is a thing...no one remembers its face anymore.

The best would be
that time would stop
right now,
in this middling moment of awfulness,
before the very worst arrives.

We'd all be spared more than telling.
That would be best.

(Pause)

GOTCHLING: The most profound thing about you, Husz, is your
irresponsibility. *(She heads for the door.)* Open the windows, clear the
air. I have work to do. A broadsheet we're putting out. The United
Front. And I'm late. *(She exits.)*

(End of scene)

Third Interruption:
Berlin 1990: The Politics of Paranoia

*(*ROLAND *is asleep on the floor.)*

ZILLAH: *(In a soft voice)* Sssshhh. Don't wake him up. He got worn
out. We were having German lessons. Listen: "Das Massengrab."
Mass grave. "Die Zeit war sehr schlimm." Times were bad.
"Millionen von Menschen waren tot." Millions of people were dead.
People try to be so fussy and particular when they look at politics,
but what I think an understanding of the second half of the twentieth
century calls for is not caution and circumspection but moral
exuberance. Overstatement is your friend: use it. Take evil: The
problem is that we have a standard of what evil is, Hitler, the
Holocaust—THE standard of absolute evil, and why? Because it's so
clear. So stark. Most other instances of evil are more veiled, hidden,
the trails are better covered, they're harder to see. So as standards
of evil go, this is more than adequate. But then everyone gets frantic
as soon as you try to use the standard, nothing compares, nothing
resembles—and the standard becomes unusable and nothing
qualifies as Evil with a capital E. I mean, how much of a Nazi do you
have to be to qualify for membership? Is a 25% Nazi a Nazi or not?
Ask yourselves this: It's 1942; the Goerings are having an intimate
soiree; if he got an invitation, would Pat Buchanan feel out of place?
Out of place? Are you kidding? Pig heaven, dust off the old tuxedo,
kisses to Eva and Adolf. I mean like a certain ex-actor-turned-
president who shall go nameless sat idly and I do mean idly by
and watched tens of thousands die of a plague and he couldn't even
bother to say he felt bad about it, much less try to help, but still be
reasonable, why should you expect the President of the United States

to be anything other than a complete moral reprobate? I mean do you have to pile up some magic number of bodies before you hit the jackpot and rate a comparison to you-know-who? Why isn't one body enough? Or fifty? Or just the likelihood, the intention enough, like is this some sort of Olympic event, handicapping Holocausts, and if it is an Olympic event I hope someone's got a bronze medal set aside for George Bush, Mr. How're-my-ratings?, because kinder gentler America is just about ready any second now to weigh in with a little mass murder of our own devising. I ask you—how come the only people who ever say "Evil" anymore are Southern cracker televangelists with radioactive blue eyeshadow? No, none of these bastards looks like Hitler, they never will, not exactly, but I say as long as they look like they're playing in Mr. Hitler's Neighborhood we got no reason to relax.

(ROLAND *stirs in his sleep.*)

ZILLAH: I never relax. Moral exuberance. Hallucination, vision, revelation, paranoia, gut-flutters in the night— the internal intestinal night bats, their panicky leathery wings— that's my common sense. I pay attention to that. Don't put too much stock in a good night's sleep. During times of reactionary backlash, the only people sleeping soundly are the guys who're giving the rest of us bad dreams. So eat something indigestible before you go to bed, and listen to your nightmares.

(*End of scene*)

Scene Thirteen:
Welcome

Slide: JANUARY 30, 1933. THE HOURS BEFORE MORNING.

(AGNES, HUSZ, *and* PAULINKA. *It's the last hour of real darkness before dawn.* AGNES *has been cleaning up.* PAULINKA *has been sobering up.* HUSZ *has been drinking.*)

AGNES: A year ago we were better people. It's evil, what's happening. Maybe you were right, Paulinka.

PAULINKA: I doubt it. Right about what?

AGNES: The Devil.

HUSZ: Sssssshhhhh!

AGNES: What?

HUSZ: I don't like loose talk about...that. Especially late at night.

AGNES: You're joking. No one really believes in the D....

HUSZ: Want to meet Him?

AGNES: Sure. Why not? You know Him?

HUSZ: Not well, but He'll come if I call.

PAULINKA: You have impressive connections, Husz.

HUSZ: My family comes from the High Carpathians, a village way up on a wild, barren mountain. Goatherds: mean, tough people. In the fourteenth century nearly everyone in the village was butchered, put to the axe for engaging in intimate congress with the Devil. Since then every Magyar born on the mountain has a special understanding with Him. He's very fond of us. He'll come. Should I...

AGNES: I already said yes.

HUSZ: Paulinka?

PAULINKA: Of course. I thought I'd have to wait till I died.

HUSZ: First you both have to cover your left eye with your hand.

AGNES: This is silly, Husz. I don't like this.

HUSZ: Quiet please. It's too late. I've already called Him.
Cover up, Agnes. *(He stands suddenly.)* Good. *(Pause)* Music ready?

(There is an answering blast of music: the finale from Mahler's second symphony [The Resurrection]. AGNES reacts violently. PAULINKA seems delighted.)

HUSZ: Lights ready?

(The lights become dim and, well, infernal.)

HUSZ: Devil...?

(From offstage and everywhere, a deep voice answers in a whisper— "Ready.")

HUSZ: Then lights! Camera! Action!

(Blackout. Then two red eyes appear, glowing. It is the Devil's dog. A strange light begins to fill the room. All the furniture has been rearranged. A great oak chair, upholstered in crimson velvet, its armrests writhing

serpents, has appeared in the center of the room. Crouching beside it, the Devil's dog, which looks like a mammoth Dresden china figurine with fiery red eyes; smoke dribbles from its mouth. The door swings open and the Devil enters. He is dressed elegantly, walks with a limp [clubfoot] and a cane, and he breathes heavily, almost asthmatically.)

HERR SWETTS: Why have you called me?

HUSZ: Thank you for coming. I hope your journey wasn't long.

HERR SWETTS: Not long, no. I have taken up temporary residence in this country. Why have you summoned me?

HUSZ: Friends of mine sensed your presence, wanted to meet you, face to face. This is Agnes Eggling....

HERR SWETTS: *(To* AGNES*)* Madame. Charmed.

AGNES: *(Terrified, speechless)* Uhhhh, ahhh...

HUSZ: And this is Paulinka Erdnuss.

HERR SWETTS: *(To* PAULINKA*)* Ah yes. I've seen your films.

PAULINKA: Monsieur, je suis enchanté.

HERR SWETTS: Et moi aussi. *(To* AGNES*)* And you, you are also in films?

AGNES: Uhhh, ahhh...

HERR SWETTS: Can she speak?

HUSZ: Usually.

HERR SWETTS: Good. Curing mutes is a messy business. What happened to your eye?

HUSZ: Knocked out by a rifle butt. Hungary, 1919.

HERR SWETTS: That I can fix. May I?

HUSZ: Free of charge?

HERR SWETTS: Oh no, no, never that, never that. A small fee, naturally...

HUSZ: Thanks, but perhaps not.

HERR SWETTS: As you wish. *(He becomes slightly more asthmatic, seems a little worried.)* Well! So! You have lovely friends, Husz. May I go? *(He starts for the door.)*

HUSZ: Oh please, not so abruptly. Leave us a souvenir.

HERR SWETTS: *(Becoming rather angry)* What? Stink of pitch that clings for years? Hair snarls? I don't dispense souvenirs.

HUSZ: Tell us something.

HERR SWETTS: I don't know anything. *(Again starts for the door, now audibly wheezing and in evident discomfort)*

HUSZ: A great mystery. The awful secret of these awful times...

HERR SWETTS: But really! I know nothing! My ignorance is beyond calculation. It springs from an abysmal font deeper by leagues than the deepest wisdom. I do not know the workings of the universe. I only know myself.

HUSZ: That, then.

HERR SWETTS: Autobiography? *(The wheezing lessens slightly.)* It's interminable.

HUSZ: Condense it.

PAULINKA: Yes, please.

HERR SWETTS: *(Slight pause, then to* AGNES:*)* Might I trouble the mistress of the hearth for a glass of wine? *(On the last words he is hit by some kind of intestinal pain. He heads for the chair.)*

AGNES: I...I...

HUSZ: I'll get it.

HERR SWETTS: Many thanks. And perhaps...a little something...for my dog. *(Again the pain)*

*(*HUSZ *pours a glass of wine, brings it to the Devil, who swallows it in one desperate gulp, then drops the glass as he doubles over in terrible pain. He begins to shake and utters a low, dreadful noise, halfway between a moan and a growl. The growl breaks into a shriek as he clutches his heart and begins to speak. His words and his physical pain are a single thing.)*

HERR SWETTS: In brief: I recall a past, nomads, seeming
to them a desert tyrant, with a petty
tyrant's heart,
cruel, greedy, englistened with fat,
fond of the flesh
of children....

(Again the intestinal pain; he now seems to be having some awful bowel affliction, alternating between diarrhea and constipation. It gets worse as he speaks.)
Years pass;
an agrarian phase, I am
rougher, reptilian,
a heart of mildew, dung-heap dweller,
fly-merchant, cattle-killer,
friend...of lunatics.
Excremental Principle, the Shit King!
(There is some kind of release/relief.)
Quaint.
Children's stuff.
Years pass, more years,
refinement, scholasticism,
increasingly metaphysical inclinations
shape me as
a negativity, a void,
the pain of loss, of
irreconcilable separation from joy, from
God!
(The heart pain returns, worse than before.)
My heart
a black nullity
from which no light escapes,
not an "Is" so much
as an "Isn't".
(The heart pain appears to have stopped.)
Too ethereal. Lacking bite.
(He stands. He appears to be getting stronger.)
Years pass, years pile up,
the last century
my heart was a piston-pump,
my veins copper tubing,
hot black oil coursed through them,
steam turbines roared.
Very strong! Very hungry!
Flesh of children and much, much more...
Heady days! The best in aeons!
(He is now standing erect, breathing deeply but without difficulty for the

first time. He mops his brow, straightens his clothing, pats his hair.)
Even that grows old.
Even yet, years hurtle by.
And in this century, still new,
when questions of form
are so hotly contested,
my new form seems to be
no form at all.
I am simply
unbelievable. Nonobjective.
Nonexistent. Displaced.
Stateless. A refugee.
The accumulation of so much,
the detritus of so many weary years,
I have at last attained
invisibility.
It's not the danger that you see
that's the danger.
I become increasingly diffuse,
like powdered gas taking to air,
not less potent, but more,
spreading myself
around.

(Slight pause)

PAULINKA: Excuse me. This is fascinating. Did you ever consider the possibility that you might be the product of neurotic conflicts? Dr. Bloom says that....

HERR SWETTS: No. My rejection of investigation is complete. I preserve my wickedness in its pristine condition. It is never touched. *(As if confiding a secret of which he is immensely proud)* I gave birth to Myself.

(PAULINKA laughs, charmed. The Devil laughs with her.)

PAULINKA: This isn't meant as an insult, but isn't that a little grandiose?

HERR SWETTS: Grandiose? Ha! Ha! Ha! That's good! Ha! Ha! Ha! Ha ha ha hahahahaha...

(His laugh turns into a loud, grotesque, subhuman braying noise which makes everyone move as far from him as he or she can. When he stops, he has lost some of his polish and is as we first saw him—foul-tempered, slightly asthmatic, uncomfortable. He points his cane at PAULINKA *and says angrily:)*

HERR SWETTS: My dear woman, you cannot possibly begin to imagine how grand...the scope of what's ahead. *(Lowers cane)* I sense great possibilities in the modern world. The depths... have not been plumbed. Yet. I haven't talked so much in years.

PAULINKA: And you really are the Devil?

HERR SWETTS: I... My card.

(He hands PAULINKA *a business card.)*

PAULINKA: *(Reading it)* Herr Gottfried Swetts. Hamburg. Importer of Spanish Novelties.

HERR SWETTS: *(Beginning to leave)* For the time being. Now please excuse me. I really must go.

HUSZ: Of course. Thank you for coming.

HERR SWETTS: *(Leaving)* Not at all. Take care, Husz. Mind the other eye.

AGNES: Wait!

HERR SWETTS: What?

AGNES: I...I...

HERR SWETTS: What?

HUSZ: Agnes, don't keep him waiting.

AGNES: I...wanted to say...thank you...for coming and...welcome to Germany...and....

HERR SWETTS: Thank you, Madam. And thank you for having me. Most gracious. Goodbye. *(He exits as the last chords of Mahler's second symphony explode and the lights go to black.)*

INTERMISSION

ACT TWO

Slide: FEBRUARY 27, 1933. NIGHT.

Scene Fourteen:
Der Mensch ist nicht gut— Sondern ein Vieh!
(Man Isn't Good— He's Disgusting!)

(There is an orange glow in the room, coming through a window from outside. All other lights are off. DIE ALTE is sitting in a chair at the table, grinding away. Two very loud knocks come from the wall. AGNES enters, turns on a light, and stares at DIE ALTE.)

DIE ALTE: Two knocks.

AGNES: The hot water pipe. It pours grey water. They have to fix it.

DIE ALTE: Little goblins, penny-men. Knock, knock.

AGNES: Oh, that poem. Funny to hear it after all these years; I can still recite it.

DIE ALTE: Memory is like the wind. Tricky. Horrible things forgotten overnight. Pleasant nothings remembered for years.

AGNES: When the tree is black and bare,
And the barren branches droop,
Don't go to the kitchen where
The penny-man makes poison soup.

DIE ALTE: When the little penny-man
Bangs the pots and pans about,
No one dares to go downstairs,
No one dares to throw him out.

AGNES: *(Sniffing)* There's that smell again. Have you noticed it in your—where you live? Something rotten, like egg or sulphur gas—maybe something died in the walls. *(She sniffs and tries to locate the smell.)* Tonight it's stronger. Smells... burnt. *(She goes to the window.)* Oh. There's a fire. A building's burning, down in the center. The whole sky's orange. Must be a terrible fire. It's one of the government buildings, with a dome...you can't see.... *(She opens the window to get a better view.)*

DIE ALTE: When God is good the hours go,
And the sun will melt the snow.
Nothing ever comes that can
Help the little penny-man.

AGNES: *(Closing the window)* It's the Reichstag.

DIE ALTE: Do you have any rolls tonight?

AGNES: The Reichstag is burning.

(End of scene)

Slide: FEBRUARY 27, 1933. A MYSTERIOUS FIRE.
Slide: THE REICHSTAG BURNS.

Fourth Interruption:
Berlin 1990: Night Bats

ZILLAH: Spooky. Recently when I have succumbed to sleep, my dreams are invaded by a woman dressed in a frumpy hat and coat—and for a change it's not Mom. This woman—I think she came from a book I read—a photograph of a huge crowd, thousands of people, a rally, everyone, and I mean everyone giving the fascist salute. But there she is, right in the middle of all these ecstatic people waving their hands, and she isn't cheering, not even smiling, and both hands are clutching her purse and she isn't saluting. I noticed her right off and I guess out of gratitude she came to pay me visits. She's in trouble: She looks old, but she isn't, she's gotten fat and her feet are giving out and her eyes are bad.

I'm here to find her. This particular ghost—proof that the past is present, if not corporeally then at least ectoplasmically. She still can't sleep. Restless, like me. I'm calling to her, across a long dead time: to touch a dark place, to scare myself a little, to make contact with what moves in the night, fifty years after, with what's driven, every night, by the panic and the pain....

(End of scene)

Scene Fifteen:
Further Demonological Explorations

Slide: FEBRAURY 27, 1933. LATER THAT NIGHT.
Slide: THE REICHSTAG IS BURNING.

(AGNES *with* MALEK *and* TRAUM. MALEK *has a carton.* TRAUM *is looking out the window.*)

TRAUM: It's still going. They should have it out by now.

MALEK: These are things we found at the party office. We think they're yours. We wanted them out before we get closed down.

AGNES: They won't dare to....

MALEK: Absolutely. Any day.

TRAUM: Arrangements have been made. We're ready.

AGNES: For what?

TRAUM: Exile.

AGNES: And then what?

TRAUM: We continue to agitate for the revolution. From without. We wait for fascism to run its course.

AGNES: Which could take how long, do you think?

(*No one answers her.*)

MALEK: (*Taking the red baby out of the carton*) Look.

AGNES: Want it?

MALEK: Burn it. Burn everything. But don't be seen doing it. Why did you stop coming around? It's months since...you disappeared. It's not a reproach, I just wondered.

AGNES: Oh, well...me? I...well I don't know. (*Pause*) When the winter set in, and it got cold. I think there's something wrong, I don't sleep. And this arm, all ice, for...hours. It's terrible. Never mind. When I turn up you know lots of people must be hearing you because I'm always the last to hear. When I disappear, I just...couldn't anymore. I'm sorry.

(*Little pause*)

TRAUM: The history of our party over the past few years has not been a happy one.

MALEK: For which thank the Comintern. For which thank Moscow.

TRAUM: Malek, please...

MALEK: For which thank ourselves for being stupid...

TRAUM: Malek, stop.

MALEK: For letting the Russians run our revolution!

TRAUM: Enough!

MALEK: Coward!

TRAUM: Not here!

MALEK: Not ever! Doing little errands while the Comintern...

TRAUM: You are appalling! Now is not the time to be attacking the only place on earth where a communist revolution has succeeded. Blame it on the German working class. Sheep and cattle! Blame it on our own inability to organize! Blame it on the Social Democrats...

MALEK: The Social Democrats the Social Democrats! They didn't kill the United Front. We did! Everything determined by what would serve Moscow best. "Hitler may be a fascist but so what, he's less likely to attack Russia than a bourgeois government allied with France!" They think.

TRAUM: So I suppose instead we should've campaigned for Hindenburg! Or we should have followed every thug who wanted to turn the Party into the Left answer to the brownshirts. Fight the Nazis on the streets.

MALEK: YES! YES! NOW! SMITE FASCISM WHEREVER YOU MEET IT! Can't you see we're already there? Don't you see how completely overdue....

AGNES: Quiet! Please!

MALEK: Sorry.

AGNES: I have neighbors. The old lady upstairs is a....

MALEK: Sorry.

TRAUM: Excuse us, Comrade.

MALEK: Enough.

TRAUM: We'd better go.

MALEK: Burn everything. Books, pamphlets, everything. But at night. Sift through the ashes. Be careful. *(Exits)*

TRAUM: Were you a Party member?

AGNES: No. Not. I was going to, but...no.

TRAUM: Consider yourself lucky. They have the members' lists. *(He starts to leave.)*

AGNES: I'm...I'm sorry.

TRAUM: Don't apologize. It's not your fault, is it? Just do what the comrade says. Burn it all.

(End of scene)

Slide: MARCH 5-MARCH 15, 1933.
Slide: THINGS GO FROM BAD TO WORSE
Slide: IN NO TIME AT ALL.
Slide: THE GERMAN COMMUNIST PARTY IS OUTLAWED.
Slide: DAILY ARRESTS.
Slide: THE EMIGRATION BEGINS.

Scene Sixteen:
Keep You Keep You I Am Gone Oh Keep You in My Memory

Slide: MARCH 5, 1933.

(AGNES is cleaning. PAULINKA is heard rushing up the stairs. She bursts through the door.)

PAULINKA: AGNES! AGNES!

AGNES: What! Paulinka, what?!

PAULINKA: *(Weeping, falling to the floor)* The worst, worst imaginable...

AGNES: Who? Who?

PAULINKA: Who what?

AGNES: What?

PAULINKA: WHO WHAT?

AGNES: WHO'S DEAD?

PAULINKA: Dead? Who said anyone died? No one died.

AGNES: From the way you're acting I assumed that....

PAULINKA: No. No one dead. It's worse than that. The death of love, the death of trust, is worse than death.

AGNES: What are you talking about?

(PAULINKA screams, a long, loud wail. AGNES rushes over and claps her hand over PAULINKA's mouth.)

AGNES: Have you gone crazy screaming like that? Do you want to have me evicted?

PAULINKA: I got there at 11:30. Tuesday morning, 11:30. I rang his bell. Nothing, nothing. Ring ring, nothing, nothing. The landlady comes out. Waddle waddle. "Oh Miss Erdnuss, it's just too awful, the Herr Professor Doctor. He's gone."

AGNES: Dr. Bloom?

PAULINKA: Poof.

AGNES: Oh. I'm sorry.

PAULINKA: SORRY! Who gives two shits if you're sorry! My analyst leaves me without a word, without the courtesy of a final session or a note or anything, right in the middle of everything he just kicks out the tent poles and leaves with his wretched wife and brats and leaves me, me! That miserable fraud, I'll ruin him. RUIN HIM!

AGNES: Shut up! Think what you're saying. Why do you think he left? Why?

PAULINKA: He had no right!

AGNES: Why? Because he's a Jew, that's why, because Germany's not safe for Jews, because....

PAULINKA: THIS IS NO WAY TO TERMINATE TWO YEARS OF ANALYSIS!

AGNES: Oh you are being selfish and disgusting. Think about him!

PAULINKA: Think about me!

AGNES: I'm tired to death of thinking about you, you, you, I don't want to anymore!

PAULINKA: Well thanks so much and to hell with you too! I'll bet he cleared out his bank account! Bet he took his money! *(She hears herself. Little pause.)* Couldn't he at least have told me?

AGNES: Of course not. Obviously not. He had to leave secretly. It's not easy to get out.

PAULINKA: I don't know what I'll do.

AGNES: Smoke a pipe. Kill tonight. It'll look better tomorrow.

PAULINKA: No, I don't think it will. This came today. It's a letter from the Ministry of Culture.

(PAULINKA offers the letter to AGNES, who does not take it.)

PAULINKA: The film industry is going to be...what was the word? *(Consults letter)* Oh yes; incorporated. I am invited to meet with the officer in charge, to discuss my plans. They like my work. *(Little pause)* They think I have a part to play. *(Pause)* Should I go? What should I do?

AGNES: I don't know. Don't ask me that.

PAULINKA: Will you work for them? Make films for them?

AGNES: I don't know. No. Maybe. No one will care if I do or not. With you it's different. What would Dr. Bloom say?

PAULINKA: Nothing, probably, he never said much. No, let's see. He'd say, "Come, Miss Erdnuss, my darling, come. Meet me in Paris or New York, the strange city they've driven me to. Come find me there. And leave Berlin." That's what he'd say. *(AGNES and PAULINKA look at each other.)*

AGNES: I don't know. I don't know what to do.

(End of scene)

Scene Seventeen:
Hic Domus Dei Est Et Portae Coelis
(This is the House of God, and These are the Gates of Heaven)

Slide: MARCH 12, 1933.
Slide: THE FLAG OF THE WEIMAR REPUBLIC
Slide: IS ABOLISHED.

(AGNES *is sitting for a portrait that* GOTCHLING *is constructing.* AGNES *holds a red hammer and a carpenter's level.* GOTCHLING *works with a pencil, paper, and a variety of assemblage materials. As she works, they talk.)*

AGNES: I don't feel like doing this today.

GOTCHLING: I know. I appreciate it all the more.

AGNES: There's no point to this. No point to making posters, they just rip them down. Don't they arrest people for this?

(No answer)

AGNES: I walked to the studio yesterday. All the way I felt like I was walking through a strange city, not Berlin. That strange sun not the Berlin sun, too bright. I found myself saying an old prayer for protection.... I keep thinking that maybe it wouldn't have been so bad to have been a wise old lady-in-waiting for the Kaiserin. In the films I had lots of well-made objects to handle: a big sturdy clothes brush with stiff bristles, Belgian lace, and there were those silver cases with little enamelled hunting scenes on the lids. They were cold but they warmed in your hand and they were heavy. Just holding them made you feel safe. What's so great about democracy? Want to see a jolly twinkle?

GOTCHLING: Please, that's nauseating.

AGNES: I know you think I'm a reactionary for feeling this way, you judge everyone all the time, but I feel that....

GOTCHLING: Feel feel feel feel feel. So much feeling. Hold still. Don't feel. Think for a change.

AGNES: There's nothing to think about.

GOTCHLING: There's plenty.

AGNES: Nothing pleasant.

GOTCHLING: Unpleasant then. We need apartments. *(Pause)* We need apartments. Belonging to people who are sympathetic.

AGNES: We who?

GOTCHLING: The Party.

AGNES: The Party's been outlawed.

(Pause)

GOTCHLING: As I was saying. We need apartments. Waystations to the east. Storage rooms...

AGNES: No.

GOTCHLING: Not for storage, then. A waystation. There are people hiding....

AGNES: No.

GOTCHLING: Agnes.

AGNES: People shouldn't be leaving. They should be staying. Everyone is going. There should be fighting. Who's going to fight? What are people like me supposed to do if people like you just leave?

GOTCHLING: Some of us are staying. Some can't.

AGNES: Are you leaving?

GOTCHLING: I can't say.

AGNES: You are. I knew you would. For God's sake, Annabella, what is going to happen to us?

GOTCHLING: I don't know.

AGNES: And still you recklessly ask me to....

GOTCHLING: Not recklessly.

AGNES: It sounds dangerous.

GOTCHLING: It is dangerous.

AGNES: Then I won't do it.

GOTCHLING: The Party needs it.

AGNES: There is no Party! There's no more Party! Wake up! You're a painter, not a politician, you always were a painter so start acting like one!

GOTCHLING: How do I do that, Agnes?

AGNES: Leave me alone!

GOTCHLING: No. I've never been that kind of a painter. Art...is never enough, it never does enough.
   We will be remembered for two things: Our communist art, and our fascist politics.

(Pause)

AGNES: I don't understand you, Gotchling. You navigate this. You're the only one. Why is that?

GOTCHLING: I'm much more intelligent than the rest of you.

AGNES: Then why do you bother with us?

GOTCHLING: I enjoy feeling superior.
Listen, Agnes.
I am working class.
And that really does make a difference. I know what's useful,
and what isn't.
I know the price of things,
and I know how to give things up.
I know what it is to struggle—
these tough little lessons
I don't think you people ever learned.
I hold tight, and I do my work.
I make posters for good causes.
Even if they get torn up, I make them,
even though we live in a country
where theory falls silent in the face of fact,
where progress can be reversed overnight,
where the enemy has stolen everything, our own words from us,
I hold tight, and not to my painting...not only to that.
Pick any era in history, Agnes.
What is really beautiful about that era?
The way the rich lived?
No.
The way the poor lived?
No.
The dreams of the Left
are always beautiful.

The imagining of a better world,
the damnation of the present one.
This faith,
this luminescent anger,
these alone
are worthy of being called human.
These are the Beautiful
that an age produces.
As an artist I am struck to the heart
by these dreams. These visions.
We progress. But at great cost.
How can anyone stand to live
without understanding that much?

Think it over, Agnes. We need the apartment.

(End of scene)

Fifth Interruption:
Berlin 1990: Vergß es, Vergieb!
(Forgive Me, Forget!)

(ZILLAH and ROLAND are having a seance.)

ZILLAH: *(To* ROLAND*)* Hit it.

ROLAND: *(Reading)* Heilig Wesen! Gestort hab 'ich die goldene Götterruhe dir oft, und der geheimeren, tiefern Schmerzen des Lebens hast du manche gelernt von mir.

ZILLAH: Anything? Anything? *(She thumbs through a pocket LaRousse German dictionary.)* Geist? Ist da eine Geist in zu Haus? Hallo? Wer ist da? More.

ROLAND: *(Reading)* O vergiß es, vergieb! Gleich dem Gewolke dort vor dem friedlichen Mond, geh 'ich dahin, und du ruhst und glanzest in deiner Schone wieder, du süßes Licht!

(A pause. AGNES *is in the apartment. The two women sense each other's presence.)*

ZILLAH: Sssshhhh.

ROLAND: Die Mäuse?

ZILLAH: Ja, ja. Eine Maus.

Sometimes at nights now I hear her moving around, sort of shuffling, patching cracks, moving things, looking for some lost object.

(AGNES *moves to the cupboard, opens drawers, looks out the window.*)

ZILLAH: Heavy steps, hardly the heart to move her feet. I ask her what her name was.

(AGNES *stops moving, looks around the room, sensing something.*)

ZILLAH: She stops moving, so I know she hears me. No answer. I ask her how she died.

(AGNES *stops moving completely, frightened.*)

ZILLAH: An air raid? In the camps? Because I know she died then, unhappy. Again, she doesn't move, and she hasn't answered me yet but when she does I already know what she'll say: "Not in the camps, and not in the war, but at home, in front of a cozy fire, I died of a broken heart."

(AGNES *gasps.*)

AGNES: Hello? Hello? Who's.... Oh dear God I need to sleep.

(AGNES *flees from the room.* ZILLAH *rushes to where she heard* AGNES *gasp.* ROLAND *sneaks up behind* ZILLAH.)

ROLAND: Boo!

ZILLAH: (*Screams, then*) Oy oy oy vey is mir! Meshuginah kraut!

(*End of scene*)

Scene Eighteen:
Berliner Schnause (Berlin Lip)

Slide: MARCH 15, 1933.

(AGNES, HUSZ, *and* BAZ. BAZ *is standing, wearing an overcoat and cap.*)

BAZ: Three days ago I was arrested by the new police. They marched into the institute after lunch. We were ordered into trucks. Dr. Henni and Dr. Kunz got into black cars. No one knows what happened to Dr. Kunz. He may be dead.

AGNES: Oh my God.

HUSZ: Want a drink?

BAZ: Oh, that would be completely welcome. I have a story.

AGNES: Are you all right? Is the institute closed?

BAZ: Boarded shut. We were accused of printing pornography and abetting illegal medical practices—abortions. The files were taken. That's bad news. We weren't prepared. Boards on the windows now. Did I say that already?

AGNES: Are you sure you're all right?

BAZ: I cried during the interrogation.

HUSZ: Lots of people do.

BAZ: But it's different when I do it. The mascara runs.

AGNES: But did they...do anything to you?

BAZ: One of them slapped me. It was more of a shock than painful. They scream a lot. Then they let us go—half of us, just turned us loose on the street, no explanation, no word about the others.

AGNES: When did they let you go?

BAZ: Two days ago...or three? Yes, three.

AGNES: Three days ago? But where have you been? Gotchling's been looking...

BAZ: I went to Munich.

AGNES: Why Munich?

BAZ: To kill myself. Really. I'm very much afraid of them, I have been for years, all police, but these are much more frightening. Being alone with them in a room with a locked door is paralyzing. I looked at the carpet the whole time. I thought, good, they have a carpet, they won't do anything that would get blood on the carpet. When the main one grabbed my face and slapped it I started crying. *(Pause)* I have always been terrified of pain. He said to me, "In the woods outside of Munich, do you know what we are building?" I said no, and he said "A camp. For people like you." I have a criminal record, I can't get out easily. I expected them to arrest me immediately after letting me go—something they do. So I decided to kill myself.

HUSZ: In Munich.

BAZ: I wanted to go to another city so that none of you would be asked to identify me afterwards. I took the night train. When I got there I bought a revolver and four bullets. Extras. I can't imagine why I thought I'd need extras. Anyway, I wanted to be found by people who aren't particularly frightened or upset by death. Nuns who care for the terminally ill. Better that than in some cafe, ruining some waiter's whole day...

HUSZ: You are wonderfully considerate.

BAZ: I try to be. But I felt that killing myself in the midst of a bunch of nuns was probably a much more serious sin than doing it discreetly in a secular location. So I went to the park.

AGNES: And...?

BAZ: Agnes, I met a remarkably attractive young Silesian there. I was exhausted. Fatigue makes me easy to arouse....

HUSZ: So you did it in the bushes.

BAZ: Husz, you are a man of the world.

HUSZ: After which you decided not to die.

BAZ: I realized after my Silesian friend left that it had been nearly a week since my last orgasm. Too much pent-up energy. The result: depression. Add to it the nightmare of the last few days—suicide. One brisk interlude with a pliable friend and my desire to live returned to me in all its hot, tainted glory.

AGNES: And so you came home?

BAZ: No. There's more. The best part.

AGNES: More?

BAZ: Well, here I am in Munich with a little money, a loaded gun, and a whole day to kill before the night train to Berlin. What to do?

AGNES: Hang around the bushes.

BAZ: No, Agnes. Once a day, every day, not too seldom, not too often, balance is everything. I went to the cinema. And you are absolutely not going to believe what happened.

HUSZ: You saw a film.

BAZ: Yes, of course, but not only that.
  It was a Dietrich film. And there was hardly anyone there, it being early in the day, just me and some old people and some war vets. When all of a sudden into the theater marches a squadron of brownshirts and guess who else?

HUSZ: Ummm...Adolf Hitler.

BAZ: Right.

(There is a pause.)

AGNES: You're making this up.

BAZ: I am not. It was him. In a slouch hat and a trenchcoat. And someone else with him, a man I didn't recognize.

HUSZ: I don't believe this.

BAZ: Well I told you you wouldn't but it's perfectly true. Hitler. And he sat down three rows in front of me. The SA sat in back of him but I had a clear view of the back of his head. I could see the oil in his hair.

AGNES: Oh my God.

BAZ: Just what I said. The film got going and I was thinking to myself, "Life plays funny tricks. Here we are, watching a Dietrich film: ten pensioners, six war cripples, Adolf Hitler, and me, a homosexual Sunday anarchist with a loaded gun in his pocket." *(He shapes the gun with his fingers, aims carefully, and makes a soft "bang".)* So I left.

HUSZ: You what?

BAZ: I left. *(Another pause)*

HUSZ: Is this true?

BAZ: Yes, it is.

HUSZ: It's true? Adolf Hitler?

BAZ: Yes.

HUSZ: And you left?

BAZ: I left.

(HUSZ *jumps up, runs over to* BAZ, *grabs him by the shirtfront, and begins shaking him furiously.*)

HUSZ: WHY DIDN'T YOU SHOOT? YOU HAD A GUN! YOU FUCKING IDIOT! WHY DIDN'T YOU SHOOT!

(AGNES *grabs* HUSZ, *who shoves* BAZ *away and storms to the opposite side of the room.*)

AGNES: Husz! Please, stop yelling, what are you saying, he....

HUSZ: What am I saying? What am I saying? Why didn't he shoot? I would have shot! Why? (*Running back to* BAZ *but not touching him*) WHAT IS THE MATTER WITH YOU?

BAZ: Because, Husz. Because they would have shot me.

AGNES: Baz, you're making all of this up.

BAZ: No. I couldn't get my hand to move, to even begin to move towards the pocket that had the gun. Because I might have killed him, but they would certainly have killed me. And I don't want to die.

HUSZ: Adolf Hitler!

BAZ: I do not want to die.

(HUSZ *turns his back on* BAZ. *There is a pause.*)

BAZ: A friend is arranging a phony passport and visa. They'll be ready in six days. I'm leaving. That's what I came to tell you. I'm leaving.

Slide: MARCH 15, 1933.
Slide: OPENING CEREMONIES
Slide: DACHAU CONCENTRATION CAMP

(*End of scene*)

Slide: MAY 1-JUNE 22, 1933.
Slide: THE TRANSITION TO FASCISM
Slide: GATHERS INCREDIBLE SPEED.
Slide: THE 150-YEAR-OLD GERMAN LABOR MOVEMENT
Slide: VANISHES OVERNIGHT
Slide: WITH ALMOST NO RESISTANCE.
Slide: THE SOCIAL-DEMOCRATIC PARTY IS OUTLAWED.
Slide: ALL MEANINGFUL AUTHORITY IS CONCENTRATED

Slide: IN THE HANDS OF THE CHANCELLOR.
Slide: IF THE SYSTEM IS NOT IN FACT COMPLETE & TOTAL,
Slide: THE ILLUSION OF TOTALITY IS ENOUGH.
Slide: THE NAZIS CONTROL NOT ONLY THE FUTURE
Slide: BUT THE PAST AS WELL.
Slide: CENTURIES OF PROGRESS SEEM
Slide: NEVER TO HAVE TAKEN PLACE.

Scene Nineteen:
Der Wildgewordene Kleinbürger
(The Petit-Bourgeois Run Amok)

Slide: MAY 1, 1933.

(The apartment is dark. DIE ALTE *staggers drunkenly about the room, clutching a bottle. She turns on the radio. It warms up, but plays nothing but static. She bangs violently on the table, three times, then shouts.)*

DIE ALTE: So it's Ho! for the man with the iron nails
And the slippery tongue so black.
With his foul breath and his hands, bang bang,
All asweat on the damp dirty bed, bang bang,
As he pulls at your hair, and he claws at your back,
And he tickles your neck and your crack, bang bang,
And he tickles your neck and your crack.

*(*AGNES *rushes in during this.)*

AGNES: This has got to end! What do you want here?

DIE ALTE: I had a black pillow once....

AGNES: *(Heading back to the bedroom)* I can't listen to this anymore!

DIE ALTE: I HAD A BLACK PILLOW ONCE ON MY BED AND I HAD HORRIBLE DREAMS!

*(*AGNES *is listening.)*

DIE ALTE: Horrible, every night. It's the black pillow, they'd warn me, you can't sleep peacefully with your head resting on that. But I loved that pillow. I'd have thrown the whole bed out before I'd throw that black pillow away. I held onto it for years.

AGNES: And the dreams?

DIE ALTE: Every night for years.

AGNES: What happened?

DIE ALTE: I wound up all alone.

(Small pause)

AGNES: I'm afraid of you.

DIE ALTE: You look green. *(She holds her bottle toward* AGNES.*)*
I'd offer you some but it's mine. Beer. German beer. Not vodka like
you and your Bolshevik friends drink.

(Small pause)

AGNES: My friends aren't....

DIE ALTE: *(Suddenly, in a rage)* BOLSHEVIK! BOLSHEVIK! FUCKING
BOLSHEVIK PIGS, ALL OF YOU! This nest; I know! You'll be
reported....

*(*AGNES *grabs a broom, which is standing nearby.)*

DIE ALTE: If you strike me with that I promise you you'll wish you
hadn't.

AGNES: *(Putting the broom down)* Who are you?

DIE ALTE: A bad dream.

AGNES: Get out!

DIE ALTE: I live here!

AGNES: This is my apartment!

DIE ALTE: Mine!

AGNES: Mine! You have no right to be here!

DIE ALTE: I'm hungry, do you have any....

*(*AGNES *grabs the old woman and begins to drag her toward the door.* DIE
ALTE *suddenly becomes very strong, and the two women begin to struggle.)*

AGNES: Let go of me let go...

*(*DIE ALTE *wraps* AGNES *in a fierce embrace, which transforms as* AGNES
stops struggling into a tender, enveloping hug. DIE ALTE *rocks* AGNES *in
her arms.)*

DIE ALTE: *(Softly)* There there there there... Kicking and fighting.
How silly it is. Feel better now?

AGNES: *(Softly)* Yes. Better. Please let go.

DIE ALTE: *(Whispers)* Time is all that separates you from me.

(The radio static flares up and then begins to play Bach's Unaccompanied Violin Sonata in G minor.*)*

DIE ALTE: Some dance. Nice music. It's bad to be too much alone.

(End of scene)

Scene Twenty:
An Acid Morning Light

Slide: MAY 2, 1933.

(The next morning. HUSZ is in a chair, bloody face, clothes torn. PAULINKA is pouring herself a stiff drink. AGNES stares at HUSZ.)

HUSZ: You see, there was a little riot....

PAULINKA: At the studio.

HUSZ: They closed down the electricians union. Some of the electricians didn't understand that. It got very ugly and everyone left....

AGNES: But you didn't.

HUSZ: LEAVE?! I WANTED TO FILM IT! And I wanted to hit someone! A whole gaggle of fascists surrounded me in a stairwell and they had their little sticks at the ready....

PAULINKA: They nearly killed him.

HUSZ: Nearly. They were interrupted by one of Germany's minor celebrities....

PAULINKA: Minor? I resent that!

HUSZ: Crying "Leave that man alone!" She marched up out of nowhere, goes to the biggest ugliest one, says "Klaus! This is beneath you!" and she slaps him. Pow! He drops his little stick, rubs his face, and says, "My name isn't Klaus." And then he looks at the other Nazis, and they walked away, completely ashamed of themselves.

PAULINKA: The performance of my career. Wasted on a crazed Hungarian and three Nazi thugs.

HUSZ: Five.

PAULINKA: Three, Husz. Three. Five and I would have pretended not to know you.

AGNES: *(Having a hard time piecing this story together, to* PAULINKA:*)* "Klaus, this is beneath you"?

PAULINKA: It's a line from the film I'm doing. Just popped out. The slap too. If I hadn't been drugged all morning I'd never have done it. *(To* HUSZ*)* They're going to come after you for this. God help you. I have to go.

HUSZ: Of course you're terrified. It makes sense to be terrified. But to stand up to the terror! Resistance! That is a great thing.

PAULINKA: I was there, Husz, at the studio to tell Special Propaganda Chief Otto Von Something-or-other that I would be interested, yes, in accepting his offer of continued employment within the film industries of the Third Reich. And you distracted me. So shit on you and your stupid moral dilemmas. *(Slight pause)* Oh, and here. *(She takes a big kitchen knife out of her purse and stabs it into the table top.)* This is yours. *(She leaves, slamming the door.)*

HUSZ: Germans...are full of surprises.

AGNES: *(Looking at knife)* I don't understand this....

HUSZ: You don't? Really? It's a butcher knife. I carry it around with me these days, hoping I'll run into someone...with ideological differences, and I'll make him see the point, as it were.

AGNES: I don't want that thing in my house. I don't want you here with that.

HUSZ: History repeats itself, see, first as tragedy, then as farce. When I was young....

AGNES: I don't want you here!

(Pause. He looks at her.)

HUSZ: Then I'll leave.

AGNES: Go!

(HUSZ stands, pulls the knife out of the table top so roughly it splinters the wood.)

AGNES: My table! You bastard! Get out! Go!

(HUSZ *starts to limp to the door, then sits heavily on the floor, unable to walk.*)

AGNES: Go! Go! Go!

HUSZ: I can't.

(*Pause. Then* AGNES *sits on the floor as well.*)

(*End of scene*)

Scene Twenty-one:
Love Scene Without...

Slide: MAY 2, 1933. LATE.

(HUSZ *is seated, without a shirt, linen wrapped around his ribs.* AGNES *is sweeping.*)

HUSZ: It will not be hard to leave Berlin. You can't imagine how much I miss Hungary. You can't imagine how much I hate German cooking. You can't imagine what it's cost me to be a castaway here, making German films, churning out the kind of bad dreams a drug addict or a criminal lunatic has before he wakes up and does something terrible.

AGNES: Husz...

HUSZ: Sssshhh. Justice...is vanishing. Like all the air in the earth's atmosphere getting used up, like life's blood running freely on the ground, pouring from a wound too big to stop up; you watch it spill, watching yourself die. Justice precedes beauty. Without justice, beauty is impossible, an obscenity. And when beauty has gone, what does a cameraman do with his eye?

AGNES: I think we should go to the hospital.

HUSZ: Get me my coat, I have something for you.

(AGNES *gets his coat.*)

HUSZ: (*Producing two packets of official-looking documents*) There. One for me, one...

(*He hands* AGNES *a packet. She looks at it, places it on the table.*)

AGNES: I didn't apply for a visa.

HUSZ: Counterfeit of course, but eminently serviceable. I have cousins in Chicago. There's a boat from Denmark, five days from today. I want you to come with me.

AGNES: I want you to go to a doctor.

HUSZ: When I lost my eye in 1919, it was the doctor who treated it who turned me in.

AGNES: You're hurt.

HUSZ: You have done extraordinary things with this bedlinen bandage. And I seem to be able to walk.

AGNES: The foot is broken.

HUSZ: No, I don't think so. Just very badly bruised.

AGNES: *(Softly)* I can't go, Husz.

HUSZ: Why not?

AGNES: I don't speak English. I can't function in strange places. It took me years to get a contract, what kind of work would I do in Chicago? Travelling upsets me. Really. I can't move. I can't move. I'm sorry. Later, maybe....

HUSZ: This is no time, Agnes, for alliances that aren't portable.

AGNES: Stay.

HUSZ: I can't.

(Pause)

AGNES: Leave then. Throw your life away. But don't expect to find anything waiting for you when you come back.

HUSZ: Goodbye, dear heart. I promise to write.

(He embraces AGNES, *tries to kiss her. She pushes him away.)*

HUSZ: It will not be hard to leave Berlin. But it will be very hard to leave you.

(End of scene)

Scene Twenty-two:
Hands

Slide: MAY 3, 1933.

(AGNES *is sitting alone at the table. She picks up the visa* HUSZ *has left behind. She tears it in half.*)

AGNES: *(Holding up her right hand)*
With this hand
I
hold water,
stir the soup,
crack walnuts,
turn keys,
scratch,
move, divide,
replace,
light the light,
write postcards,
pay,
receive payment,
grasp,
fill out a ballot, seal it,
take up a knife,
make a cut.
The practical hand,
this hand,
its veins, nerves, tissue,
and bones.
Five fingers has this hand.
With five I can....
(Holding up her left hand)
Now this hand.
With this hand,
weak claw, I
shred shadows,
brush dust,
drop glass, let go,
sense changes in the air by
the subcutaneous twingings,

the shy retirement of heat
to cool inner safety;
this hand to make
a frail moon-cup
protective patch
over the weak eye,
the eye that cannot bear to see.
Five fingers has this hand.
With five I can....
(Holds up right hand)
And this is the hand that betrays me.
(Holds up left hand)
And this is the hand that holds my life.

(End of scene)

Sixth Interruption:
Berlin 1990: Treffpunkt (Turning Point)

ZILLAH: Airplane ticket.

ROLAND: Lufthansamaschine.

ZILLAH: Auf Wiedersehen.

ROLAND: Goodbye.

ZILLAH: What a year, huh? Germany re-unites, Russia has a famine, and America starts World War III. And they say God has no sense of humor. I have to go. I've met my doppelganger. Here. *(She points to her heart.)*

ROLAND: Herz.

ZILLAH: Finish the story. See it through to the end. And then go home.

ROLAND: Heim. Wohnung. New York City. Phantastisch.

ZILLAH: Neo-refugee. I go where things are falling apart, not coming together; I don't wanna be a settler, I wanna be an un-settler. Head for the bad weather, the turbulent air. Where the night-bats fly. Where you can see the danger.

(AGNES *enters.*)

ZILLAH: *(Seeing* AGNES*)* ...if there's safety anywhere, it's there.

*(*ROLAND *leaves. From this point till the end of the play,* ZILLAH *remains onstage, watching the final events.)*

(End of scene)

Scene Twenty-three:
Revelations and Farewells

Slide: JUNE 22, 1933.

*(*AGNES *stands near the window, looking out.* PAULINKA *is dressed for travel.* BAZ *is in a chair, his coat and valise nearby.)*

PAULINKA: The train ride to Moscow will take three days. The trip to Hollywood would have taken a month. So I decided to go to Russia. Well, not really. The Americans found out about my old KPD membership.

BAZ: Remarkable.

PAULINKA: What kind of a world is it where Husz moves to America and I wind up in the USSR? Doesn't that seem...backwards or something?

BAZ: Don't talk about Husz when you get to Moscow. Don't say you knew him. Stay out of politics.

PAULINKA: Easy for me to do.
   There was this woman in Wardrobe who used to fold a KPD leaflet very carefully and slip it into the pocket of my costume on the sly. Every once in a while. Then she'd wait for me to find it, and when I did she'd be watching, and she'd wink at me. I hated her. Last week, I guess someone informed on her; they came for her at the studio. She screamed. But... That was it for me. I faked a nervous breakdown, or maybe I didn't fake it, who knows. And so on. The end.
   You're being ominously quiet, Agnes. You could at least wish me a pleasant voyage east.

(Pause. AGNES *looks at* PAULINKA, *then out the window again.)*

BAZ: The winters in Russia have a nasty reputation.

PAULINKA: I packed my fur. And I expect a warm welcome in Moscow. I, too, have a reputation. It isn't so terrible. They do make the best films.

BAZ: Not recently.

PAULINKA: Don't be so morbid, Baz. Put a good face on it.

BAZ: Hard to do.

PAULINKA: Apparently. Not for me. Frightening, isn't it? What an actor does. Assume the mantle of truth, of courage, of moral conviction, and wear it convincingly, no matter what sort of chaotic mess there is inside.
Agnes, you have to say something.

AGNES: You...are going to miss your train. I wish you'd go now. Please go.

(Pause. PAULINKA leaves.)

AGNES: See? You'd think, when a person goes, a whole person just goes away, it would leave a hole, some empty place behind, that's what I thought, I imagined that, but...it doesn't. Everyone's going but it isn't like the world has gotten emptier, just much smaller, more closed in. It contracts, the empty places...collapse. Goodbye.

BAZ: Plans? What are you....

AGNES: Sssshhhh. Goodbye. Please.

BAZ: Goodnight, then. Paris awaits.

(BAZ reaches in his pocket, takes out an orange, places it on the table.)

BAZ: Weather this, Agnes. And keep the door locked. *(Exits)*

(End of scene)

Slide: JULY 14-17, 1933.
Slide: ALL LEGISLATIVE AND POLITICAL WORK
Slide: NECESSARY FOR THE ESTABLISHMENT
Slide: OF THE THIRD REICH HAS BEEN COMPLETED.
Slide: THE FASCIST MACHINERY CREATED IN SIX MONTHS
Slide: WOULD FUNCTION EFFICIENTLY
Slide: FOR THE NEXT THIRTEEN YEARS.

Scene Twenty-four:
All That Was Fat and Bright is Perished from You

(GOTCHLING *and* AGNES)

AGNES: What do you want?

GOTCHLING: That's quite a welcome.

AGNES: I haven't seen you for months. You must want something.
I thought you'd gone for good.

GOTCHLING: I have, officially.

AGNES: Officially where?

GOTCHLING: Officially Switzerland.

AGNES: And really where?

GOTCHLING: Switzerland.

AGNES: Lie.

GOTCHLING: You don't want the truth.

AGNES: Lie.

GOTCHLING: It doesn't matter. I need your help. The apartment...

AGNES: I knew it. The answer's no.

GOTCHLING: There's no one else. You have to.

AGNES: I do not. You can't make me risk my life. Risk your own.

GOTCHLING: I am.

AGNES: Good for you. How wonderful. I refuse this honor.

GOTCHLING: Tell you what. We'll make a deal.

(*No answer*)

GOTCHLING: You can't save yourself, Agnes. If you make it, you
make it, but only because you're lucky.

AGNES: I don't know what you're talking about.

GOTCHLING: You will. If you say no to this, Agnes, you're dead to
me. And we both need desperately to keep at least some part of you
alive. Say yes, and I promise to carry you with me, the part of you
that's dying now. I can do that, I'm stronger than you. Say yes, and

I will take your heart and fold it up in mine, and protect it with my life. And some day I may be able to bring it back to you. You're very fond of regrets, Agnes, but the time for regretting is gone. I need very much to be proud of you.

AGNES: If I get arrested, Annabella Gotchling, I swear to God I will never forgive you.

GOTCHLING: Three days from now, around six in the evening. Expect her. She says she knows you. Her name is Rosa. *(Exits)*

(End of scene)

Seventh Interruption:
Berlin 1990: Lullaby

(ZILLAH and AGNES alone)

ZILLAH: There's a terror that skips
over the mind and out the throat
faster than thinking:
Revelation: We
are in danger.
It catches us by surprise,
on beautifully sweet evenings
when we're most thoroughly
at home,
and says look
for the cracks
where the seams don't meet,
look where the walls
have moved slightly apart,
try to see, stay awake,
there isn't time for sleeping.
(She whispers to AGNES:)
Horen? Kannst du mich horen?
Before the sky and the ground
slam shut.... Now. *(There is a knock at the door.)*

(End of scene)

Scene Twenty-five:
The Green Front

(There is a soft knock at the door. The knock again. AGNES goes quickly to the door, opens it a crack, then lets ROSA MALEK in.)

AGNES: No one saw you.

MALEK: No.

AGNES: How can you tell? There are so many doorways and alleys and windows.

MALEK: I don't think anyone saw me.

AGNES: You don't think? Oh God in Heaven...

MALEK: You've got to calm down. What if someone saw me? I'm not wearing a red beret and a sign saying "Escaping Communist."

AGNES: But later, when they come looking—I shouldn't have done this, I really shouldn't. It's no joke. Goddamned Annabella. They'll find out. The hateful people in this building. They get money for informing.
   Calm, calm. I need a drink. Do you want a drink?

MALEK: Yes, please.

(AGNES pours two glasses—it's wine now, not vodka—and gives one to MALEK. They both sit.)

AGNES: But you can't stay here long.

MALEK: Just till morning.

AGNES: Morning. And then you've got to leave. And don't give this address to anyone else.

MALEK: No.

(Pause)

AGNES: *(Calmer, softer)* Where are you going? After here?

MALEK: I can't say.

AGNES: No, well, no, that's...that makes sense. I wouldn't actually want to know. But...you'll still be...working.

MALEK: I really can't talk about that.

AGNES: No. Please, I'm sorry. You probably think I'm a spy. I...
I haven't changed that much. I just need to know that you'll be
working. You and Gotchling. You'll keep doing what needs to
be done, underground, I couldn't, I'm not really worth much,
I suppose...the fear is too great, it makes me stupid, but...it still
matters to me.

MALEK: I know it does, Agnes.

AGNES: And this will pass. Months, not years.

MALEK: There are people working, and it will pass. But it could be
years.

AGNES: Oh no, not years, I don't think so.
   I'm afraid of living alone, here, that something will happen to me.
Stupid of me telling you this, you have such real things to be
frightened of but...I'm lonely. And years frighten me. I ought to do
something to help but I'm simply not able. The arrests. Every day
they execute....

MALEK: *(After a brief pause)* This is important. What you've done for
me.

AGNES: *(Suddenly angry)* This is nothing. Don't coddle me. This is shit.
   I think we should go to sleep. *(She gets up and goes toward the
bedroom.)*

MALEK: Agnes.

(AGNES stops but does not look at MALEK.)

MALEK: On the border, in Karlsbad, there's a house: 30 Erzegebirge
Street. Memorize the address, don't write it down. 30 Erzegebirge,
like the mountains. The front of the house is in Germany. The back
of the house is in Czechoslovakia. The people who live there are...
friends of ours, and the Nazis don't know about it yet—the system
is full of little holes like this. Go there by train, at night, if it gets bad
here; knock on the door and tell them you're looking for the Green
Front. They'll take you to the back door, and you're out. If you need
to. Ask for the way to the Green Front. The borders are full of holes.

(AGNES walks slowly to the bedroom without looking back.)

AGNES: Please be gone by morning.

(She closes the bedroom door. End of scene)

Epilogue

(AGNES, *alone at the kitchen table. She has an orange, which she pushes, causing it to roll off the table and across the floor.* DIE ALTE *enters through the bedroom door, picks it up, and begins to peel and eat it.* ZILLAH *watches.*)

AGNES: I live in a modern flat.
On one side lives nightmare,
on the other despair.
Above me, exhaustion,
below me, a man
with the pale face
and red hands
of a strangler.

DIE ALTE: I can eat anywhere. I remember
the thick smoke rising from the ruins of home,
black plumes in an ash-white sky,
the sun transformed
into a nickel-plated dot
no bigger than a groschen. It seemed
to race through the clouds—
or was that the moon? No.
The sun. The moon
was huge and rusted
like an infected eye.
It moved slowly, and the nights were black.
Rats looked for bodies under the rubble,
so corpses had to be torched right in the street:
a piteous sight.
The planes came back
every day
to bomb the craters they'd created
only the day before.
The water was oily
and full of typhus.
Everyone was patchy,
delirious, diseased,
and waiting for the end....

AGNES: When God is good
The hours go,
But the world rolls on,
Tumbrel-slow,
And the driver sings
A gallows-song:
"The end is quick.
The way is long."

I fear the end
I fear the way
I fear the wind
Will make me stray
Much farther than
I want to stray
Far from my home
Bright room called day;
past where deliverance or hope
can find me.

DIE ALTE: But through it all
I never lost my appetite,
and never ceased to look for food,
just like the rats.
I ate while the bombs fell,
ate while the bodies burned,
ate at the funerals, hurried and undignified,
of people I had loved....
Ate
through days of pain
and nights of terror;
with cracked teeth
and split lips
I kept eating, digesting,
and looking for meals.

When they rounded us up,
and brought us to the camps,
and showed us the mass graves and said,
"You
are responsible for these."
I was thinking, "I

wasn't here,
didn't know,
didn't want to know,
never pulled a trigger,
never pulled a switch,
feel nothing for these beds
of sleepers, deep asleep,
but only
look at how thin they are,
and when they let us return to Munich
I wonder what I'll find for dinner."

(The room begins to grow dark.)

ZILLAH: Home. Now. An end to the exile.
Before the sky and the ground slam shut.
The borders are full of holes.

AGNES: Club-foot.
Smell of sulphur.
Yellow dog.
No shadow.

Welcome to Germany.

THE END

TRANSLATIONS FOR ROLAND'S LINES

First Interruption

Pages 23-24:

Beethoven, ja. Er ist in der Stadt geboren, in der ich geboren wurde.
Beethoven, yes. He was born in the same city I was.

Freiheit. Super.
Freedom. Super.

Ich denke, Beethoven ist da geboren. Jedenfalls, ich bin es. Weißt du
wo Leipzig ist?
I think Beethoven was born there. Anyway, I was. Do you know
where Leipzig is?

Ich bin total doof. Ich habe nie Englisch lernen konnen. Französisch
auch nicht.
I'm a total moron. I could never learn English. French either.

Second Interruption

Pages 41-42:

Vielleicht sollen wir 'was essen gehen. Indisch?
Maybe we should go for food. Indian?

Ich bin noch jungfraulich. Außerdem, bin ich Sozialist, ich bin nicht
nach dem Westen gefahren, um Tennisschuhe zu kaufen, aber ich
würde schon gern mal bumsen.
I'm still a virgin. Anyway, I'm a socialist, I didn't come to the West to
buy tennis shoes, but I would like to get laid.

Ich glaube, ich sollte dich warnen, ich bin vielleicht bisexuel. Ich
fühle mich schwindlig.
I think I should warn you, I may be bisexual. I feel dizzy.

Reagan?
Reagan?

"Mister Gorbachev, tear down this wall!"
Ich hab 's im Fernsehen gesehen.
I saw it on TV.

Fifth Interruption

Page 68:

Heilig Wesen! Gestort hab 'ich die goldene Götterruhe dir oft, und
der geheimeren, Tiefern Schmerzen des Lebens Hast du manche
gelernt von mir.
Holy Being! Often have I disturbed your golden, god-like repose, and
the secret, deeper pains of life, some of which you have learned from
me.

O vergiß es, vergieb! Gleich dem Gewolke dort Vor dem friedlichen
Mond, geh 'ich dahin, und du Ruhst und glanzest in deiner Schone
wieder, du susses Licht!
Oh forget, forgive! The clouds before the peaceful moon, I go there,
and you rest and shine in your beauty again, you sweet light!

*(Note: The preceding poem is by Holderlin, and this translation is
grotesquely literal.)*

Die Mäuse?
Mice?

THE ILLUSION

freely adapted from Pierre Corneille's

L'ILLUSION COMIQUE

THE ILLUSION

THE ILLUSION is for Brian Kulick,
collaborator and friend.

ORIGINAL PRODUCTION

THE ILLUSION was first presented by New York Theater Workshop in October 1988, directed by Brian Kulick, with the following cast:

PRIDAMANT .... Victor Radier-Wexler
THE AMANUENSIS .... Stephen Spinella
ALCANDRE .... Isaiah Whitlock, Jr
CALISTO/CLINDOR/THEOGENES .... Michael Galardi
MELIBEA/ISABELLE/HIPPOLYTA .... Regina Taylor
ELICIA/LYSE/CLARINA .... Socorro Santiago
PLERIBO/ADRASTE/PRINCE FLORILAME .... Neil Maffin
MATAMORE .... Arthur Hanket

The play was subsequently performed, in the current expanded version, at Hartford Stage Company in January 1990, directed by Mark Lamos, with the following cast: Marco St John, Jarlath Conroy, Frederick Neumann, J Grant Albrecht, Ashley Gardner, Bellina Logan, Andrew Coulteaux, and Phillip Goodwin.

It was next produced at the Los Angeles Theater Center in April 1990, directed by David Schweitzer, with the following cast: Alan Mandell, Tom Cayler, Mary Woronov, Jonathan Silverman, Lea Thompson, Karole Lynn Foreman, Mitchell Lichtenstein, and John Fleck.

CAST

PRIDAMANT of Avignon, a lawyer
THE AMANUENSIS, servant to ALCANDRE (also GERONTE)
ALCANDRE, a magician
CALISTO/CLINDOR/THEOGENES, son of PRIDAMANT
MELIBEA/ISABELLE/HIPPOLYTA, beloved/wife of CALISTO/
    CLINDOR/THEOGENES
ELICIA/LYSE/CLARINA, maid/friend of MELIBEA/
    ISABELLE/HIPPOLYTA
PLERIBO/ADRASTE/PRINCE FLORILAME, rival of CALISTO/
    CLINDOR/THEOGENES
MATAMORE, a lunatic

The play takes place in the cave of the magician ALCANDRE during the 17th Century, near Remulac, a small town in the south of France.

Author's note: This version of L'ILLUSION COMIQUE was done for a production directed by Brian Kulick, who brought the play to my attention and asked me to adapt it. It owes much of its present structure and texture, as well as one of its best jokes, to him; Mark Lamos (the Emperor of Ice Cream) and Connie Congdon also provided great dramaturgical advice, inspiration, and concrete ideas; Nina Mankin was invaluable in getting it into playable shape; and it owes its second life to Greg Leaming's support. My deepest gratitude to them all.

ACT ONE

(A man alone in a dark cave)

PRIDAMANT: Is this the cave of the magician Alcandre? *(Silence)* Is this.... Nothing here. Hello? *(He strikes a match; it fizzles out.)* Hello!

*(*THE AMANUENSIS *appears, dressed in black, silent.)*

PRIDAMANT: Is this the cave of the magician Alcandre? I'm a pilgrim in need of his services.

(Pause. No response from THE AMANUENSIS.*)*

PRIDAMANT: Is your master in? Can you speak? I followed the directions carefully, but I've arrived.... *(Looks around, shrugs)* I shouldn't have come at night, I suppose, but to be honest I'm ashamed to be seen in a place like this, wizards and spells, I...I'm Pridamant of Avignon. *(Pause)* That name means nothing to you. Well, it means something in Avignon. Assure your master I can pay. More than adequately.

(Again a pause. THE AMANUENSIS *is silent and still.)*

PRIDAMANT: Say something! Move, fetch, announce me, more light or... Very well, I must have the wrong address. A thousand pardons and good night.

*(*PRIDAMANT *turns to leave.* THE AMANUENSIS *knocks loudly on the floor.)*

VOICE: He doesn't speak because he has no tongue.

*(*PRIDAMANT *freezes. Another knock.)*

VOICE: And because he's deaf he didn't catch your name.

PRIDAMANT: Pridamant. Of Avignon. I'm looking for the sorcerer Alcandre they told me lives in this dismal pit.

VOICE: Turn around.

(PRIDAMANT *does.* ALCANDRE *appears.*)

ALCANDRE: What do you want from him?

PRIDAMANT: Do I have the honor....

ALCANDRE: What do you want? This is close enough; my time is precious to me; your business, or go away.

PRIDAMANT: I want a more intimate consultation.

ALCANDRE: Furtive whispering.

PRIDAMANT: It's something personal.

ALCANDRE: So ashamed...

PRIDAMANT: I'm not ashamed of anything.

ALCANDRE: Then why not declare your business openly?

PRIDAMANT: *(Pausing, then, referring to* THE AMANUENSIS*)* Is he really deaf and dumb?

ALCANDRE: I did the surgery myself. I too have need of privacy. He is my servant; I keep his tongue in a jar. He serves me devotedly, all the better since I had his eardrums pierced. You are a troubled and unhappy man. What crimes have you committed? Confess.

(Pause, then)

PRIDAMANT: I destroyed my son. My only child. Years ago. When he was barely a step past being a boy. He seemed uncontrollable, wild, dangerous to me in all sorts of little ways. I loved him so much I wanted to strangle him. I wanted to snap his spine sometimes in a ferocious embrace. Everything about him seemed calculated to drive me to distraction, and did.

ALCANDRE: You murdered your son?

PRIDAMANT: I might have; he ran before I had the chance. Disappeared. Helped himself to as much money and as many valuables as I'd left unlocked and fled Avignon, and that was fifteen years ago. Since then I've never had a word from or about him; hired agents could unearth no trace; expensive information proved worthless; I have paid through the nose for every clue but always I am led to a blank, tall, doorless wall through which he seems to have slipped. As if by magic.

ALCANDRE: Magic. Which explains your long journey from Avignon to me.

PRIDAMANT: It's near-fatal for a man of my age and poor physical condition, I never thought I'd make it. I hear you can.... They tell me that you conjure. That you can bring to bear on any situation certain skills and lost arts of a pre-Christian variety....

ALCANDRE: Even if I could restore your son to you I wouldn't. He's lucky to have escaped....

PRIDAMANT: But I've changed. For the first time this year in the early spring I faced death in the form a sharp, surprising tearing at my heart. A warning. Nothing of my life for the past fifteen years is real to me. I can't stop thinking about him. I can't face death until I see him again. I want to tell him I love him. I want to ask him why he never wrote. I want him to know that the ghost of him has ruined my life, has sucked dry everything, present happiness and memory as well. I want to make him sick with guilt. I want to make him the heir to my fortunes. He must be very poor....

(Figures appear, dressed beautifully, frozen in a tableau.)

PRIDAMANT: Oh, impossible, impossible; it's him; you've called him back to me.... My heart, as I told you, I have to avoid excitement.

ALCANDRE: Odd for a man avoiding excitement to come to a magician's cave at night. What did you expect?

PRIDAMANT: Information. Memory restored. I don't know. But safely, painlessly. Crystal balls and tea leaves, not this...resurrection.

ALCANDRE: You're perfectly safe here.

(The tableau shifts. PRIDAMANT *moves away quickly.)*

ALCANDRE: Frightened?

PRIDAMANT: My son always frightens me. I want to speak to him.

ALCANDRE: Uh uh uh. Violate the boundary between their world and ours only at the greatest peril to yourself. Cross over, and you may not be able to find your way back.

PRIDAMANT: Then what am I to do?

ALCANDRE: Use your eyes, your ears, take from their carryings-on whatever you can, these clouds of colored vapor. Resign yourself, a fitful sleeper in the throes of a nightmare, powerless to affect his life, a possibility you relinquished years ago.... If he teeters on the brink of some fatal trap you can call out a warning, still he'll fall in and die.

PRIDAMANT: I wouldn't want to see that.

ALCANDRE: I'll show you his life, just as he's lived it, since you cast him off. How it ends, I cannot say.

PRIDAMANT: He's so young. He's hardly aged at all.

ALCANDRE: Before the night is through, he will. You see him now as the young man you banished, years ago. Life is still fresh to him. Full of wonders...

CALISTO: I have seen a most splendid vision.

PRIDAMANT: What's he talking about? Is he also a magician?

ALCANDRE: He is frequently in love.

CALISTO: The vision's name is Melibea.

ALCANDRE: *(Pointing to* MELIBEA*)* That one there. Your son's great passion, his waking dream. If we retreat, the first phantasma can commence.

CALISTO: I was hungry;
I trapped a hawk, a little wire snare
Snatched it by the red foot and I said
"That's dinner."
But it pleaded with me not to eat it, high heart and all,
So I released it after making a pact:
"I set you free; you find me other prey."
And I let go and in a panic it tore madly away;
I followed it; it led me here,
To your garden, Melibea,
More wonderful than freedom, or the air itself,
Where with the hungry eye of a hawk
I am watching your every move. My love.

PRIDAMANT: At home he always told stories like that. When I could catch him I'd whip him for telling lies.

CALISTO: This garden wall encircles paradise;
Within, Melibea waits; if I touch the stones

I can feel her heart beating, and I know, I know
It's beating for me.
Melibea, Melibea,
Open the door of your garden wall.
It's cold out here, I'm freezing.

MELIBEA: It isn't cold, it's spring, and warm,
And I know who you are,
Calisto.

PRIDAMANT: Calisto? His name's not....

MELIBEA: You can't come in.

CALISTO: I'm in already.

MELIBEA: Only the sound of you—eventually
Your voice will give out.

CALISTO: My voice in your garden; my words in your ears....

MELIBEA: My fingers in my ears; I'm deaf to your prayers.

CALISTO: My words will linger till they spy a chance,
When your guard is lowered, to shower you with love.
Your voice is honey, even your contempt,
A sweet potent liquor I draw into my roots, then
I sprout green leaves atop my head
And blossom purple buds of desire for you.
Out here, Melibea, look out here,
Don't you want to see such a miraculous plant?
Come and shelter under me: I am a Melibea-Tree.

MELIBEA: You're silly and you're poor,
Calisto; I'm too busy for your games.
You make me nervous. Please go away.

CALISTO: I'll climb the wall.

MELIBEA: I'll call the gardener.

CALISTO: And let his blood water the roses....
Let me in or I'll stab my eyes out.

MELIBEA: Leave or I'll have you arrested. I don't know you. You're
excessive. And strange. Calisto. That probably isn't even your real
name.

PRIDAMANT: It isn't! His name isn't Calisto, it's....

AMANUENSIS: *(Fiercely and rather frighteningly)* Sssshhhhh!

ALCANDRE: Sssshhh. Sit and don't move. Watch and don't talk.

MELIBEA: Calisto. Like from some old romance.

PRIDAMANT: But I must interrupt, please. Something's wrong, something's off, it looks like him but they've got the name wrong.

ALCANDRE: What do you mean, wrong? Wrong according to whom? It isn't wrong, it's what it is, it's what it has to be; Calisto, it's the perfect name for him, shapely, strong, open-ended, with a little bite, I...There are always these small discrepancies between vision and memory. Concentrate on the general outline, leave the details to me. And keep quiet.

PRIDAMANT: She thinks he's an impostor. Perhaps the new name is as false as the fancy get-up.

ALCANDRE: Yes, yes, perhaps, watch and see.

MELIBEA: You're an impostor. I'm sorry you're so miserable but it's not my fault.

CALISTO: It is, it is.

MELIBEA: I'm done with you.

CALISTO: I'll die out here.

MELIBEA: Die and decay, you garden pest. Elicia!

(ELICIA enters.)

ELICIA: Ma'am?

MELIBEA: Make sure that leper stays outside. If he tries to breech the barricades, shoot him dead.

ELICIA: Between the eyes.
(As MELIBEA exits.)
My aim is true. You can always depend on your trusty maid.
(MELIBEA is gone. ELICIA opens the garden door.)
Let's have a look.
Oh God, another one!

CALISTO: Another what?

ELICIA: Another suitor. Each day there are more. They're dropping from the trees like the apples of autumn, just as wormy, most of them are, just as over-ripe....

CALISTO: If I have rivals I have to fight them.

ELICIA: There's just one other roundabout today,
Well-bred, polite, a charming man.

CALISTO: I was trying to be charming. It didn't work. She hates me now.

ELICIA: Well...

CALISTO: She does, she does, she hates me now, I'll die, I will, I can't live without her.

ELICIA: You saw her yesterday for the very first time.
You've spoken to her twice.
You lived before you met her and
You'll live for years to come.

CALISTO: I won't.

ELICIA: You will. You look perfectly healthy.

CALISTO: I only look that way; inside, I bleed.

ELICIA: And so does she.

CALISTO: She...suffers?

ELICIA: Dreadfully.

CALISTO: Because...?

ELICIA: A man.

CALISTO: ...Who causes her pain?

ELICIA: Night and day.

CALISTO: Show me; I'll kill him; I'll tear out his heart
And offer it up as a present to her,
A savage token of my barbaric love!

ELICIA: Savage, barbaric, but not very bright!
It's you, you fool, you lunatic, you lout,
You're her persecutor, she aches for you.

CALISTO: No.

ELICIA: Yes.

CALISTO: No.

ELICIA: Yes.

CALISTO: Yes?

ELICIA: Yes.

CALISTO: Yes! How do you know?

ELICIA: Oh we maids know these things about our mistresses;
We're in and out of their lives like bees in lilies,
Tidying up more than their bedclothes and their hair.
She didn't have you arrested.

CALISTO: She threatened to.

ELICIA: But she didn't. I would have. She didn't.
You're alarming. Wild. How can she resist you?
You have such pretty teeth. Each one
Like a little kernel of white corn.
Here she comes: hide in the bush;
She's on the brink: I'll give a push.
(Aside) She's ready to fall for him head over heels;
And why am I helping? I know how he feels.
When passion possesses you freeze and you burn,
Your bedsheets get knotted; you toss and you turn;
Your laundry gets soiled, you tear out your hair,
So I'm helping out; and why should I care?
I find him attractive; and intrigue is fun,
And a surrogate love affair's better than none.

(MELIBEA enters.)

MELIBEA: Who are you talking to Elicia?
I thought I warned you to keep the door shut.

ELICIA: There's a gentleman, Ma'am.
He's lying out here. On the ground,
Writhing and flailing in some kind of mortal agony,
Making terrible terrible sounds.

MELIBEA: Oh, let me see. (She looks.)
There's no one here.

ELICIA: He's disappeared.

MELIBEA: Maybe he got better and went away. Or maybe he crawled into a bush to die. We could start beating the bushes, I suppose.

ELICIA: Spare the poor bushes. Wherever he's crawled, we'll hear him moaning. He moaned very strangely, the poor, poor man.

MELIBEA: Strangely?

ELICIA: Yes. Each moan sounded like someone's name. Yours, in fact. Just like this: "MMMMMMMelib-b-b-eeeeaaaahh!", "MMMMMMelib-b-b-eeeeeeeaaaahhh!"

MELIBEA: Oh! Oh! Calisto! It was Calisto! He's found yet another way to make a spectacle of himself! Another way to drag my name through the mud! Calisto! That troll! That fountain of dreadful metaphors! *(She kneels.)* Please, Holy Father, please, Blessed Mother of God, what crime did I commit that you should send this demon to torture me? Make him go away! He frightens me! I hate him! I hate him! I hate him I hate him I hate him!

CALISTO: *(To* ELICIA, *from the bush)* It's going very well. Congratulations.

ELICIA: *(To* CALISTO*)* Back in the bush. I'm not done yet. *(To* MELIBEA*)* I know just what you mean, ma'am. The minute I saw him I said to myself "I hate that man." For one thing, he's so ugly.

MELIBEA: Isn't he?

ELICIA: Remarkably ugly. Warty like a squash. Greasy. Fat. The ugliest man I ever saw.

MELIBEA: Well, not so ugly as that, but....

ELICIA: Ugly enough. And incredibly stupid!

MELIBEA: Stupid?

ELICIA: A veritable clod of earth; an ox could outsmart him.

MELIBEA: I thought he spoke well.

ELICIA: Sure, if you like hearing gibberish.

MELIBEA: It wasn't all gibberish.

ELICIA: Oh please, ma'am, your natural generosity carries you away.

MELIBEA: I am not naturally generous, it's just that he....

ELICIA: All that hot air! *(Imitating* CALISTO*)* "Melibea! So fair! Radiant! Divine! Beautiful Melibea! Little star of the dawn!"

MELIBEA: Actually I liked the part about the little star of the dawn.

ELICIA: You're far too sensible to fall for that stuff. I mean obviously you aren't worthy of such intense, passionate adoration.

MELIBEA: What do you mean by that?

ELICIA: Well, it's obvious.

MELIBEA: Oh really?

ELICIA: I mean you're perfectly nice and all but you're not exactly the little star of the dawn.

MELIBEA: Well he thought I am.

ELICIA: But he's a troll.

MELIBEA: No! I mean, yes, but...

ELICIA: But?

MELIBEA: But...

ELICIA: But there are worse things than trolls.

MELIBEA: Many worse things.

ELICIA: Trolls are...well, unusual!

MELIBEA: They are! And sweet.

ELICIA: Sweet, yes, maybe a little.

MELIBEA: Who? Calisto?

ELICIA: Maybe a little?

MELIBEA: Maybe...

ELICIA: A little?

MELIBEA: A little. Yes.

ELICIA: And he'd probably be better behaved and sweeter still if it wasn't for that toothache.

MELIBEA: Toothache? He has a toothache?

ELICIA: Oh, yes, didn't you know, a horrible toothache, for eight days running.

MELIBEA: Oh how dreadful. There's nothing worse than a toothache.

ELICIA: Nothing. His manservant tells me....

MELIBEA: Yes?

ELICIA: That to ease his terrible pain...

MELIBEA: The toothache...

ELICIA: The toothache.

MELIBEA: Yes?

ELICIA: He sings.

MELIBEA: Oh...

ELICIA: And plays the lute...

MELIBEA: I love the lute.

ELICIA: And that the countryside for miles around
Grows peaceful with the bright response of birds,
And, playing and singing, handsome as a god,
He isn't even Calisto anymore.
He is like Orpheus.

MELIBEA: He is Orpheus! And I am his Euridyce! Rescue me from Hell!

ELICIA: Pardon?

MELIBEA: I said I don't feel well. I'm going to my room.

ELICIA: If I see him again, maybe I could give him your handkerchief.

MELIBEA: My handkerchief?

ELICIA: He could use it to wipe his fevered brow. Or I could wipe it for him.

MELIBEA: DON'T YOU DARE! I mean, let him wipe his own brow. I mean, here.... *(Giving her the handkerchief)* I have to go to my room, I can't breathe.... *(She exits.)*

CALISTO: *(Entering from the bush)* It's strange.

ELICIA: Very strange...I did better than I expected. I nearly convinced myself.

CALISTO: It's destiny.
(*Taking the handkerchief*)
I'm the child of fortune, Elicia;
The orphan child of fate.
I was cast out; the wind blew me here
On great brown wings; and I always knew
She'd rescue me; she had no choice
But to love me.

ELICIA: I almost feel sorry for her. You look hungry.

CALISTO: Starving. But I think I'm about to be fed.

ELICIA: Ha ha.

CALISTO: Ha ha. Your eyes are pretty when you laugh.

ELICIA: You will be true to her, won't you?
I have a heart....

CALISTO: Attractively enshrined...

ELICIA: And I feel responsible since I've set her up.

CALISTO: My every thought is of Melibea.
My eyes, my eyes are all for her.

ELICIA: Sweet Calisto, your eyes are very dark.

CALISTO: Like my father's—deep, dark, there's nothing but love in them.

PRIDAMANT: That's the look! See? In his eyes! The look that said danger to me. A thousand times since the day he ran away I asked myself, "Did I imagine that look?" but there it is. It makes my blood run cold. I am glad to have seen this. His feral stare, like a wounded animal, dangerous, with teeth.... What might he have done to me if I hadn't driven him out?

ALCANDRE: He's merely in love with his Melibea. That's a look of love.

PRIDAMANT: Love, yes, but what does love mean? Nothing. Anything can be called love, any sort of emotion. I find myself enjoying this vision, this vindication. It's delectable. Memory without pain. Like eating a great deal of delicious food without the concomitant indigestion.

ALCANDRE: As if you'd lived a life you never really lived.

PRIDAMANT: It makes me feel immortal. Please, continue. I watch gluttonously.

ELICIA: I will bring her to you,
Who is yours by fate.
I think she's simmered long enough,
And should be ripe for eating. Poor little bird. *(Exits)*

CALISTO: The sun is setting!
Just for me!
The moon is rising! Just for me!
My happy heart's crawled up inside my mouth;
It lies there like a frog,
Amphibiously glad to see the night descend,
Bubbling the name of my beloved:
"MMMMMelibbbea. MMMMMelibbbea. MMMMM..."
Heaven sparkles, mad with joy,
The earth spins 'round an ache.
I am its core, its point, its pearl—
I want, therefore it spins.

(CALISTO starts to hide. PLERIBO enters. CALISTO stops. They stare at each other, at first with a kind of confused recognition, and then with growing animosity.)

CALISTO: Who are you?

PRIDAMANT: Ah, it must be my son's rival, looking for his lover; poor fool; against this sharp-billed shrike he doesn't stand a chance.

PLERIBO: Who are you?

CALISTO: Calisto. Who loves Melibea more
Than he loves himself, or God,
Or the world, or all the world's riches.

PLERIBO: Pleribo. Who loves Melibea more than that.

CALISTO: I love her so much that if she asked me to cut off my hand I'd do it.

PLERIBO: Well I love her so much that if she asked me to cut off one hand I'd cut them both off.

CALISTO: Well I love her so much that if she asked me to cut off both hands but she didn't really want me to I'd do it anyway.

PLERIBO: Well I'd do it too and I'd also cut off my feet.

CALISTO: Would you really do that?

PLERIBO: No. I mean not really. I mean, who would do something like that?

CALISTO: *(Meaning it)* I would.

(Little pause)

PLERIBO: This is a private garden. You'd better leave.

CALISTO: Make me.

PLERIBO: Uh, I forgot something inside. *(He starts to exit.)*

CALISTO: *(Stepping in front of him)* No.

(CALISTO slaps PLERIBO.)

CALISTO: If you love Melibea, fight for her.

PLERIBO: *(Near tears)* But I don't want to fight you.

CALISTO: You have to. We're rivals.

PLERIBO: That really hurt! That really hurt! You...hurt me!

(PLERIBO stares at CALISTO, then lunges at him. CALISTO knocks him easily to the ground.)

CALISTO: *(Crouching beside the prostrate PLERIBO)* I did?

PLERIBO: Yes. I've never been hit before.

CALISTO: I could keep hitting you. And it would hurt more and more. But do you know what will make the pain completely unbearable?

(PLERIBO shakes his head "No.")

CALISTO: Melibea will come through that door soon. She'll see you beaten. It hurts to be hit. It will hurt much much more to be thoroughly humiliated in front of her. Don't you agree?

(PLERIBO doesn't answer.)

CALISTO: So I'm going to turn my back, and you can leave. Better hurry, because I hear her coming down. If I turn around and you're still there, it will be very unpleasant for you. Take my word for it.

(CALISTO *turns his back.* PLERIBO *hesitates, then crawls away.*)

CALISTO: My first rival bested!
It wasn't so hard; and well-timed,
My Melibea of the moon is coming.
I'll hide and await my cue. *(He hides.)*

(MELIBEA *and* ELICIA *enter.*)

MELIBEA: Is it safe? No one here?

ELICIA: No ma'am, no sign of Ca...

MELIBEA: Ssshhhh!!! Please, for the love of God,
Speak that name only to murder me.

ELICIA: What's wrong with you, Ma'am?

MELIBEA: I have a fever. I thought the night air
Would cool it down; it makes it worse.
I hurt.

ELICIA: Where's the pain?

MELIBEA: It starts here. *(Indicates her heart)* And then it spreads
throughout. I have aches and chills in places I've never felt achy
or chilly before. Am I dying?

ELICIA: Probably not. Where God gives a wound
He also gives a remedy;
As it hurts, so it heals. I know
The very medicine for this malady.

MELIBEA: Is it a plant? Does it grow in the garden? Is it nearby?

ELICIA: Very near.

MELIBEA: Pluck it, please, and bring it to me...

(ELICIA *hands* MELIBEA *to* CALISTO.)

MELIBEA: Oh!

CALISTO: Melibea.

MELIBEA: Calisto.

CALISTO: You aren't drawing away.

MELIBEA: I can't.

(The hawk's cry is heard.)

CALISTO: Look! See that shadow flying?

MELIBEA: Oh, a hawk!
What a sound it makes.
Every animal in the whole moonlit world
Freezes when it hears that cry.
It's like an icicle through the heart.

CALISTO: Are you shivering?

MELIBEA: It's cold.

CALISTO: Melibea. The source of fire is here in me;
Put your hand on my heart.

MELIBEA: *(Does this, and then pulls her hand away)* It's like a burning
coal. How strange, Calisto.

CALISTO: You are the answer to my every need.
I'll keep you warm, you'll save me from burning;
Both winter ice and blistering sun
Will be ours to command.
The winds will blow wild over our happiness....

(They kiss. ELICIA *runs in, breathless.)*

ELICIA: You'll have to run! Pleribo's told your father!
He's arming the gardeners with shovels and spades!

MELIBEA: Calisto!

CALISTO: In my imagination and in my speeches
I have slain a hundred gardeners!
What are these real gardeners
To the monstrous horticulturists
I have vanquished?

ELICIA: For Melibea's sake, you have to flee from here!
Leave her, please, her father is dangerous, and
The Law is clear and very harsh!
For her sake, if not for yours!

CALISTO: I will return! Wait for me, my own adored!
With my great love for you...

(The theater goes completely black.)

PRIDAMANT: What happened? Magician? Hello? The visions have disappeared! Just as the father was about to enter! A light, please, I'm blind....

(There is a tick-tock noise. A dim light comes up. PRIDAMANT *is alone with* THE AMANUENSIS, *who is making the tick-tock noise with his tongue.* ALCANDRE *appears.)*

ALCANDRE: Don't be alarmed. A great leap is taking place.
Days, months, years perhaps...

PRIDAMANT: But the father was about to appear.

ALCANDRE: Irrelevant to the story.

PRIDAMANT: Your servant. That noise. He...

ALCANDRE: Yes?

PRIDAMANT: He... Why is he doing that?

ALCANDRE: To indicate the passage of time.

PRIDAMANT: But... He's making the sound with his tongue.

ALCANDRE: Yes.

PRIDAMANT: You said he doesn't have a tongue.

ALCANDRE: Now he does.

PRIDAMANT: That's impossible.

ALCANDRE: If I can bring back your son I can restore a simple little tongue. Check your pocketwatch against him; you'll find he's remarkably accurate.

PRIDAMANT: Can he hear as well?

ALCANDRE: Naturally, he'll need a functional pair of ears to effectively participate in the vision about to unfold.

PRIDAMANT: Participate? But we can't enter their world! You said....

ALCANDRE: I said it was dangerous. And it is. But it can be done. I used to do it all the time. Finally I grew too old, acquired this hobgoblin; now, when it's necessary to cross over, I fling him into the chasm instead of going in myself. Would you care to try it? Join your son in his shadowy habitation?

PRIDAMANT: Absolutely not. I'm staying here.

ALCANDRE: No, no of course not, consumption, spectation, scrutiny, not participation, a wise choice, mi padrone. We begin again.

(The tableau for Part Two appears: MATAMORE *and* CLINDOR.*)*

PRIDAMANT: My son looks different. Has he aged? His clothes are richer. No, I was wrong, it's not my son. Calisto's coming now....

CLINDOR: *(To* MATAMORE*)* Your servant, Clindor.

PRIDAMANT: Clindor? This is my son, Calisto.

ALCANDRE: You said his name wasn't Calisto. I wish you'd make up your mind.

CLINDOR: Master, it amazes me,
Titan whose countenance
Is the world's great terror,
You've scaled the loftiest
Pinnacles of glory, and still you
Dream of conquest. Do you never rest?

MATAMORE: Never, slave, and now I must decide
Whose kingdom I should next acquire,
The King of Crete's or the Queen of Britain's?

CLINDOR: Both are island kingdoms; you would need
A navy of a thousand ships and
Ten thousand men to sail them.

MATAMORE: Ships? Men? I need no ships.
I'll swim the Hellespont on Monday
And the Channel Tuesday morning. And as for troops
I need none, other than
This mighty arm...

CLINDOR: Mighty indeed!

MATAMORE: ...And this fist of tempered steel.
I crushed the hearts of the Pashas of Ranjapoor
And battered down the cypress gates of Sinabar
With little else. The splinters like spears
Slew the gate's defenders by the dozens
And with the hinges I cracked chariot and shield of
A hundred hundred knights. The blood ran
Ankle deep; it's not a thing

I like to talk about. Let Crete and Britain
Look to heaven: Matamore is near!

CLINDOR: Oh let them live, great Master, you
Have more than gold and land enough.

MATAMORE: Half the planet.

CLINDOR: More than half. I spoke before
Of conquests sweeter but
More difficult to win....

MATAMORE: You speak of Isabelle. My genius
Leaps pages ahead to grasp your meaning.

CLINDOR: I bow before your protean brow.

MATAMORE: Then speak of Isabelle, but do not speak
Of difficult conquest. I know: My visage frights
The moguls and viziers: A fearsome face,
An awful, horrible, ghastly face,
A face that has sunk a thousand ships,
And made six hundred oxen run bellowing into the sea!
But look: I can transform this mask of Mars
To something of transplendent, masculine
Yet gentle Beauty. *(He does this.)*

CLINDOR: Sorcery. You are as invincible, I see,
In battles of the heart as of the sword,
And not even the proudest woman could resist you;
Aphrodite herself would collapse at your feet.

MATAMORE: She did, in fact, and begged for me.

CLINDOR: But you spurned her.

MATAMORE: Utterly.
She interfered with my military campaigns.
Always clinging, eager for amour.
Since then I'm more careful displaying
My face of love.

CLINDOR: Temperate and wise!
But don your face, my godlike lord,
For Isabelle is near!

MATAMORE: Isabelle! You gave to her
The sonnets I indicted to her beauty?

CLINDOR: I did, my liege.

MATAMORE: And what was her response?

CLINDOR: She read them carefully, and wept.

MATAMORE: Tears of joy, no doubt. And here she comes,
I... She is accompanied by my rival;
Like a tick, he clings to her inseparably. *(Starts to exit)*

CLINDOR: Where are you going, scourge of heaven?

MATAMORE: He's a weak man, and weak men are foolish.
He might be tempted to challenge me.

CLINDOR: Then you could obliterate him.

MATAMORE: I never fight with my love face on,
I worry that it might get scratched.

CLINDOR: Put on your terrible mask of war, then, and slaughter him.

MATAMORE: What? With Isabelle so near?
Are you mad?
My mask of Mars clapped on my face
I'm fiercer than the tusked boar
And I might gore them both,
Skewering my love and rival both.

CLINDOR: I spoke rashly. Perhaps we should retire instead.

MATAMORE: Perhaps we should. I'll lead the way.

(They exit. ISABELLE *and* ADRASTE *enter.)*

ADRASTE: I have devoted myself entirely
To discovering the sight, the sound,
The word that will finally awaken you
To my devotion, the word that will set marvels free.
But nothing penetrates your shrouded heart.

ISABELLE: Those who don't understand the world
Think words have meanings that adhere
With constancy; you offer me a thing
And say it is a rose; to you, no doubt,
It is. To me it's a thistle,

And I'm pricked by its thorns.
You say you love me; I say you torment me.
You describe me at great length, and
I know you think I'm flattered;
In point of fact I'm bored.

ADRASTE: When a kind word from you
Would be life's blood to me
You're silent as the dead.
You only speak to heap scorn on my love.

ISABELLE: I only speak to tell you how I feel.
I have no more feeling for you, Adraste,
Than the dead have for anything;
I'm insensate; for God's sake
Let me rest in peace.

ADRASTE: You ought to pity me, at least.

ISABELLE: I do.

ADRASTE: And should I live on that? Pity,
When I'm ravenous for your love?

ISABELLE: You may be ravenous; I have no food to give.
I do pity you. Your pain's unnecessary and absurd.
I don't mean to bruise your tenderness
With my harshness, but please know, Adraste,
That I cannot love you, do not love you,
And want nothing other than your absence.
Only your persistence makes us enemies.

ADRASTE: Enemies. You will never be an enemy of mine,
Isabelle. I loved you long before we ever met;
We two are torn halves of one whole that existed
In some earlier, better world than this.
You defy all of heaven's designs if you refuse to love me.

ISABELLE: Then I defy them; tell heaven to stop asking me
To do impossible things.

ADRASTE: Listen to me, Isabelle.
Your father's chosen me, you know he has;
I have to have you; if not through love,

I'll invoke the Law and his paternal right
To settle your affairs as he sees fit.

ISABELLE: That's a dead end, and a desperate move.
If I'm taken as goods, traded
With a handshake and a bill of sale, I promise you
That I will poison both
Your bed and your life with my hatred of you.

ADRASTE: A quick death with you in a poisoned bed
Is better than living alone.
I'll take my chances.
Your father's walking in his garden.
I'll close the deal.
The bill of sale was drawn up long ago.

ISABELLE: Please, Adraste...

ADRASTE: You pity me.
I can't be guided by pity for you.
My love's too fierce; it won't permit me to
Pity the woman who hates my love.
I go now to claim you: my murderer; my bride.

PRIDAMANT: I'm utterly bewildered. It's uncanny. Why has everyone changed their name?

ALCANDRE: You still pick after tiny details, like a lawyer examining a brief.

PRIDAMANT: I am a lawyer. A man has a right to expect coherence....

ALCANDRE: Expect nothing from these visions you can't expect from life. I gave up hoping for coherence years ago....

(MATAMORE and CLINDOR re-enter.)

MATAMORE: Madam, do not be alarmed
To see your gutless suitor fled away.
He saw me coming....

ISABELLE: And instantly ran.
He shows better sense in this
Than I'd have guessed him capable.

CLINDOR: Kings and emperors, after all,
Would do no less.

ISABELLE: When Matamore approaches,
Everyone retreats; in fact,
I feel an urge myself....

MATAMORE: It's natural to flee me; I am so great,
At times I want to flee myself;
But stay with me; I'll extemporize
Another sonnet to your grace.

ISABELLE: Oh don't do that! I mean, not while
The sweet music of the other twelve you wrote
Is still ringing in my ears; let me savor that.

MATAMORE: You're as beautiful as you are wise!
An excess of sweetness is as disagreeable
As a lack of bitter gall. Hmmmm.
That's rather good! Delamont!

CLINDOR: Um, it's Clindor, Sir.

MATAMORE: Delamont, record that last remark.
(To ISABELLE*)* I'm collecting
My pithiest sayings in a book.

CLINDOR: *(Writing)* This one, Sir, is full of pith.

MATAMORE: Thank you. Read it back to me.

CLINDOR: "An excess of sweetness is as disagreeable
As a lack of bitter gall."

MATAMORE: My God that's good. One problem, though.

ISABELLE: What's that?

MATAMORE: It makes no sense.
Ah well, I'll have to work on it.

ISABELLE: Oh do! Polish it up, in some private place,
And give it to me as a present.
I adore a well-polished epigram.

MATAMORE: I have a thousand others....

ISABELLE: No. I want this one. Go. To work.
Your messenger of love
Can stay with me and press your advantage
While you wrestle with your muse.

MATAMORE: I will buff it to a brilliance, and make it shine
So that you can see yourself reflected in its biting wit.
Delamont...

CLINDOR: Clindor.

MATAMORE: Whatever. If the Queen of Iceland should arrive,
Tell her I am indisposed.

ISABELLE: The Queen of Iceland?

MATAMORE: Will not let me rest; pursues me in her sled;
And wants my fiery love to thaw
Her frozen marriage bed.
Also good. Write it down, Delamont,
I'm off to shine my epigram. *(Exits)*

CLINDOR: It will take several years, I think,
To make that saying shine.

ISABELLE: Then we shall have to amuse ourselves while he's away.
Can you, messenger of love, amuse me for as long as that?

CLINDOR: For several years? Without a doubt.

ISABELLE: Begin, then, I need to be amused.

CLINDOR: I'll tell you a story.

ISABELLE: Is the story fact or fantasy?

CLINDOR: Does it matter?

ISABELLE: Yes, I've heard too many fantasies today.
Tell me something true.

CLINDOR: Once there was a servant,
Without land or means or title, poor, an orphan,
Forced from his home by an unloving father,
Who found employment with a lunatic squire
To act as his bootblack, his secretary
And more. To deliver messages of love.
To a beautiful lady.

ISABELLE: This is a sad story; I'm intrigued but not amused.

CLINDOR: It gets sadder still. Can you guess
What soon befell this poor young Mercury?

ISABELLE: Tell me.

CLINDOR: He went one day to deliver a letter to the lady
And unexpectedly delivered his heart instead.

ISABELLE: Did the lady accept it?

CLINDOR: I've forgotten how it ends.
Do you think she did?

ISABELLE: Yes. I do.

CLINDOR: Even though the messenger
Had never told her of his love before?

ISABELLE: Oh but he had. With a tongue of air, a quiet voice,
That spoke truer, clearer, finer words
Than any she'd heard in all the endless vocalizing
Of a dozen braying lords. It did not brag, lie,
Flatter, or threaten, this quiet voice,
But it sang a silent hymn of adoration
Only her heart could hear.

CLINDOR: And then what happened?

ISABELLE: I suppose
They fell deeply, completely in love.

CLINDOR: The story's improving. Maybe it ends happily.

ISABELLE: Maybe. There's a rival.

CLINDOR: There always is a rival.

ISABELLE: And a father who forbids their love.

CLINDOR: Fathers, too, have a habit of becoming
The very nemeses of love.

ISABELLE: What hope for a good conclusion, then,
With obstacles like these?

CLINDOR: Obstacles are only obstacles
Until they're overcome.
In all such stories,
The lovers exchange
Some token of their passion;
Traditionally, it seems to me, a kiss....

ISABELLE: I never defy tradition
Unless I'm driven to....

(They kiss.)

ISABELLE: My father's choice is made;
Now I make mine. I love you.
My father's very strong;
I'm stronger. And I will have my way.

(ADRASTE enters.)

ISABELLE: *(To* CLINDOR*)* Tell your master I refuse his advances;
My heart is occupied with other matters;
I'll send my maid down with a letter,
Explaining the vagaries, the strange fortunes of love. *(Exits)*

ADRASTE: I can't help but envy your fortune,
Boy. Isabelle, who flees when I approach,
As though a sudden rainstorm had spoiled the day,
Was listening very carefully to you.
One wonders what you have to say to her.

CLINDOR: Only what my master Matamore
Would like me to convey.

ADRASTE: I think it would be better if your master
Took his madness and its messenger
Somewhere else.

CLINDOR: My master, Sir, is harmless;
He can't compete with you.

ADRASTE: You seem intelligent, a decent sort of man.
It's inexplicable that you should serve
This monster of ego run amok; no poverty
Or need for gold could justify this servitude.

CLINDOR: You're rich, Sir, and have never felt
The need for gold;
I respectfully suggest you have no idea
What sorts of things poverty justifies.

ADRASTE: I don't trust you; and I respectfully request
I never see you here again.

CLINDOR: It's hardly fitting, my Lord,
For you to feel so threatened by a man of my low rank.

ADRASTE: I don't feel threatened;
I've already won the prize.
Her father's signed a wedding pact with me.
Your master's a pest, but he makes me laugh.
You I don't find funny in the least.
Climbers and pretenders never are.

CLINDOR: Someday you'll be sorry you said that.

ADRASTE: Are you threatening me?

CLINDOR: No. I'm prophesying, Sir, a gift I have.
I take my leave, with your permission.

ADRASTE: Granted instantly.
And may swift winds blow you on your voyage hence.

(CLINDOR *exits.* LYSE *enters.*)

LYSE: You spoke with him?

ADRASTE: I did.

LYSE: And now you see you were mistaken.

ADRASTE: On the contrary. I'm all the more convinced.
She's fond of this servant.

LYSE: She is.

ADRASTE: That's more than you'd confess before.

LYSE: I'm sorry for you, Sir. I am. And, I admit,
I had some hand in shaping her opinion of this man.

ADRASTE: What is her opinion?
I want the truth.
Is it as bad as I think it is?

LYSE: (*Showing the letter*) You'll spare the bearer of bad news?

ADRASTE: What's in the letter you hold in your hand?

LYSE: She worships him. He's all her heart.
As much as Matamore amuses her;
As coldly as she feels towards you,

So much and more does she entirely yearn for him.
She's sick with love.

ADRASTE: Then let her sicken and die!
I'll kill her for this treason!
I...
It's disgraceful for a lady of her rank
To throw herself on paupers.

LYSE: He tells me that his father's rich,
But they're estranged; he says all sorts of things.
He pretends to be a simple sort of servant, but
He can talk like the Devil, beautiful words,
And he scatters them freely, in every direction.
He can make you forget
Where you stop and he begins,
And after five minutes conversation you find
That you're breathing in tempo with him. It's eerie.
I'm worried. For my mistress' sake.

ADRASTE: Your loyalty's impressive, Lyse. Is it for sale?

LYSE: Not on the open market, but for a good cause...

ADRASTE (*Giving her a diamond*) Will this do as a deposit?

LYSE: Handsomely. I'm all for you.

ADRASTE: I want to catch them making love.

LYSE: Easily arranged. They rendezvous down at the arbor in fifteen
minutes. You'll find them together. Will Clindor be hurt?

ADRASTE: Yes. I promise you that.
If I can return my pain to its wellspring,
I'll do it happily. And if he feels
Even a drop of what I've suffered,
He'll carry the scars till his dying day. (*Exits*)

LYSE: By this betrayal I bait the trap;
When its jaws snap shut, Clindor will bleed.
It's not for the love of a glittering stone
That I set the stage for this bloody deed....
I only seek justice, to punish a sinner—
And now comes the cat—sniffing for dinner.
I'll be a cold fury in my fatal resolve.

(CLINDOR *enters.*)

LYSE: Good morning, Sir, did you sleep well last night?

CLINDOR: Like a statue, Lyse.
I didn't stir once; the sheets on the bed
Weren't even wrinkled....

LYSE: Now isn't that odd?
When I left your room, all of the linen
Was thoroughly mussed.

CLINDOR: But after you'd gone,
I smoothed everything over;
Like magic the bed looked
Like it hadn't been touched;
And with your smell trapped
On my hands and my sheets,
I drifted off to the sweetest slumber.

LYSE: I'm glad I helped you to a good night's sleep.

CLINDOR: You have a letter. Is it for me?

LYSE: No. It's addressed
"To My One Faithful Love."
And since it's from Isabelle,
It can't be for you.

CLINDOR: Are you angry?

LYSE: Oh no. Not angry, darling Clindor;
I've discovered a new feeling,
One that has no name. My heart is full of it;
If I could make a broth,
With my heart as the meat stock
And this feeling as the spice,
One sip would curl your lips back from your pretty face
And send you straight to Hell.
But I'm not angry.

CLINDOR: I haven't been untrue to you.

LYSE: Isabelle would be surprised to hear you say that.
I'm a little taken aback myself.

CLINDOR: I love you both equally.

LYSE: Oh, what nonsense.

CLINDOR: I do, Lyse, I do. Equally, but differently.

LYSE: Equally but differently. Her sparkling eyes, my dainty foot...

CLINDOR: Your beauty, and her money.

LYSE: I see. Well, that's blunt.

CLINDOR: I won't insult you by telling you stories.
I could easily spend a century or two in bed with you. But...

LYSE: But you can't live on that. Do as you intend to do: Go where
the money is.

CLINDOR: My desire's all for you.
But all you have to offer is desire.
I do desire Isabelle, and also
All that Isabelle affords:
I'm tired of being poor.
You have nothing, I have less than that.
Two zeroes equal zero.
It's simple mathematics.

LYSE: The worst thing is,
Your schemes make sense to me.
Marry money; I'd do the same....

CLINDOR: Love in poverty's short-lived;
Poor and married we'd soon fall out of love.
You understand.

LYSE: God help me, I do.

CLINDOR: I knew you would. The letter, please.

(She gives it to him.)

CLINDOR: She'll meet me?

LYSE: In the arbor.

CLINDOR: I'll go there and wait for her.
You're so beautiful it's dangerous to stay.
My love might get the best of me
And spoil everything. *(Exits)*

LYSE: The best of you. Now there's a laugh.
I've had your best, and you've had mine,
And used me up, and cast me off; your best,
You bastard, looks to me
No better than your worst.
He thinks he's now a little God
In the golden shrine of Isabelle's heart;
I'll tip him out, this serving man,
And watch him tumble down;
As he pricks, this trickster, let him pay!
As he plays his changes on the theme of love
Oh change his pleasure into pain, and let him lose
The thread of his unholy variations! Justice
And unhappiness!
That's how it has to end.

PRIDAMANT: They're all in league against him! I don't want to watch anymore.

ALCANDRE: But he's your son. Surely you want to see how he fares in this sea of sharks.

PRIDAMANT: Not really, no. It's too upsetting, and I don't like what's going on.

ALCANDRE: But it's history, it's memory, it's all already happened, and your closing your eyes can't alter that—

PRIDAMANT: I can leave!

ALCANDRE: Oh, well, your tricky heart, I understand, the tension, you find this bit too alarming, it agitates unnecessarily—allow me to make a small adjustment....

(He motions in the air, and LYSE is struck by a sudden change of heart.)

LYSE: On the other hand:
If revenge tastes sweet, as they say it does,
Does this taste so like brass because
As much as I'd love to spoil his plan
I'm still in love with this catlike man
Whose cruelty's all of an animal kind,
A matter of muscle, rather than Mind,
And though he deserves to be knocked down flat,
There's nothing accomplished by killing the cat.

I must recant my treason,
Unravel the weave of this deadly design,
Undo what I've done....

(MATAMORE *enters.*)

MATAMORE: I have it, I have it, my epigram,
Sweet Isabelle, I....

LYSE: And for that purpose,
Here comes the very King of Undoing.

MATAMORE: Ha. Isabelle gone. Her scullion, alone.
What's become of your mistress, scullion?

LYSE: My mistress, Sir, has become....
I cannot say it.

MATAMORE: Your reticence is commendable, Jade.
But speak. You must;
For Matamore's gaping ears
Even the stumps of trees divulge
Such secrets as tree stumps possess.
Tell me, poppet, where's she gone.
That gleaming, beaming, peerless wonder?

LYSE: She's down in the arbor making love to your servant.

MATAMORE: I beg your pardon?

LYSE: Isabelle, that gleaming, beaming wonder,
Is at this moment in the arbor with your serving man,
And they're not pressing grapes.

MATAMORE: Do you mean to imply...?

LYSE: I do.

MATAMORE: Affronterous pimple!
Presumptuous homuncula!
Foul dustball, perfidious chamber-pot,
Do you mean to imply that....

LYSE: Go there, see for yourself, Isabelle and Clindor are....

MATAMORE: Poodle, cease your yap!
Trullish chambermaid, do you think
That such a gross Leviathan as myself would stoop

To spy upon my future Queen,
The soon-to-be-Empress of my limitless realms
In some seedy grape arbor with my little minion,
Thinking to catch them at illicit palaverings?
It is grotesque! It is vile!
It is loathsome!
Where's the arbor?

LYSE: Down this path.

MATAMORE: I knew that already. I am there.
Thus saying thus, swept the offended Matamore away. *(He exits.)*

LYSE: The tender scene he'll interrupt
Is better torn asunder by this poltroon
Than by poor, love-torn, and dangerous Adraste.
There still is time—
I pray that madness travels faster
Than the spirit of revenge. *(She exits.)*

(Change of scene: in the arbor. CLINDOR and ISABELLE enter.)

ISABELLE: My father's turned to stone,
A monolith on which is carved
The awful words: Adraste and Isabelle will wed.
He'd rather see me dead that married to a serving man.
It's not safe for you in this tyrant's house;
At any strange noise, we have to run.

CLINDOR: I can protect myself.

ISABELLE: Since we last met you've become as irreplaceable
As the blood in my veins, as the air I breathe,
As my dreams at night, as my memory of joy.
Protecting you, I keep myself alive.

CLINDOR: My father's house is barred to me.
I have nothing to offer you, except....

ISABELLE: Except your love, which is all I desire.
The wanderings of the heart will at last find rest,
The vagaries of love will cease,
Here, here will be home forever,
For you, for me...my only, only love.

(Leaping from hiding place, MATAMORE enters)

MATAMORE: Let Jove in heaven with thunderbolt split
This usurperous dog, this treacherous equerry! I... *(He faints)*

ISABELLE: Oh god! Is he dead?

CLINDOR: No, not dead, merely
Overcome by prolixity.
Let me talk to him.

MATAMORE: Unspeakable machiavel!
False-foreswearing Judas-lips!
Et tu, Delamont?

CLINDOR: Thunder more softly.
I beg you, dread Goliath....

MATAMORE: I have no need to shout.
You know what you have done.
A crime so ghastly I cannot bear to pronounce it.

CLINDOR: I have stolen Isabelle.

MATAMORE: Precisely. You have two choices:
One: To be seized by the heels and flung
Straight through the celestial crystalline spheres
Into an abyss where the elemental fire will consume
What parts of you remain unripped by broken crystal.

CLINDOR: Sounds bad.

MATAMORE: It is. Or Two:
To be transformed by a spell I know
Into that lowliest of creatures, the Naked Mole Rat,
Thereafter to be stepped on by my puissant boot
After which your skin will be made into a little
Ratskin purse for Isabelle to wear,
Embroidered with the words:
Thus died Delamont, traitor to his lord.

CLINDOR: Actually, there's a third choice.

MATAMORE: There is?

CLINDOR: Yes. I could beat you to a bloody pulp.

MATAMORE: I see. And which of the three will you choose?

CLINDOR: Guess.

MATAMORE: Look, you've obviously learned
A great deal from me. The ignominious deaths
I've mentioned ill-befit so well-trained
A soldier as yourself. Say you're sorry,
Promise to abjure the sight of Isabelle forever,
And we part as friends. Do you prefer that?

CLINDOR: I'd prefer to throw you in the river.

MATAMORE: I can't swim.

CLINDOR: That's too bad.

MATAMORE: Your spirit is astonishing! My warrior heart
Cannot but thrill to hear so brave a boast!
Spoken like a soldier! I am magnanimously moved;
I give her to you
As one warrior, however greater, to another warrior,
However less. I have so many lovers, I can share.

ISABELLE: It breaks my heart to lose the chance
To be your concubine, but I take solace
In knowing how relieved
The Queen of Iceland will be.

MATAMORE: She will; her ice-bound beauty,
Great as it is,
Was never match, my Isabelle, for you.

ISABELLE: Pronounce on us, colossal Matamore,
Your blessing and your benediction,
A thing my father won't provide....

MATAMORE: Let me be your father, then, if that's
The role I'm meant to play.
Pledge each other your vows.
I stand, for once, as silent witness.

ISABELLE: And I, for once, obey you, Father,
And join my heart, Clindor, to yours.

CLINDOR: Confirm that vow by giving me....

(ADRASTE and LYSE enter. ADRASTE has his sword drawn.)

ADRASTE: Your hand on hers, slave, is profanation.
Your punishment, to lose that hand.

(ADRASTE *slices the air with his sword.* CLINDOR *pushes* ISABELLE *away. The others scatter.*)

CLINDOR: *(Pulling a dagger from his boot)*
Her name upon your lips is even greater profanation;
Your punishment, to speak no more.

(They begin to fight in earnest.)

PRIDAMANT: This isn't dangerous, is it, it looks dangerous....

ALCANDRE: I'll make it disappear if it upsets you.

PRIDAMANT: *(As they fence)* No, wait, let me... Oh! Look at that! Look at him go. It's wonderful! Thrust! Thrust! Thrust! Thrust! Parry, hah! I...oh I must be careful not to get overexcited.... Wow! What technique he has, he fences like an aristocrat, elegant but not foppish, not affected, what a fighter he....

(CLINDOR stabs ADRASTE.)

ADRASTE: Isabelle!

PRIDAMANT: *(Horrified)* Oh. Oh. He's dead.

(ADRASTE dies horribly. CLINDOR *dips his hand in* ADRASTE's *blood, and tastes it, raises his hand to the sky. Blackout.)*

(The lights restore.)

PRIDAMANT: What's happened? Where's Clindor?

ALCANDRE: In prison, of course, where murderers go.

PRIDAMANT: He's not a murderer! I know the law! Self-defense, he was attacked!

ALCANDRE: He killed a nobleman. He has no means. No lawyer to defend him. It's gone badly for him, I'm afraid. The penalty is death.

PRIDAMANT: You lied to me. You said it turned out well. I feel...a dreadful little tingling in my heart. My valerian drops...

ALCANDRE: My servant will get you some water. Then he must go.

(The servant brings PRIDAMANT *a glass of water.)*

PRIDAMANT: Go where?

ALCANDRE: Across the threshhold to the other side. From here to there. He's eager to go.

(THE AMANUENSIS *does something to indicate exactly the opposite.*)

PRIDAMANT: He crosses over? He...dissolves, a cloud of vapor, like them? Does it hurt?

ALCANDRE: It exacts its price, yes.

PRIDAMANT: Then why put him through it?

ALCANDRE: My visions are concocted through a violent synthesis, a forced conflation of light and shadow, matter and gossamer, blood and air. The magic's born of this uneasy marriage; it costs, you see, it hurts, it's dragged unwillingly from the darkest pools.... I need his agony, I'm a chemist of emotions, his misery's my catalyst, it fuels my work, I regret the pain the journey causes him, I'm fond of him I suppose but...I have to keep the work interesting for myself, don't I? You can't imagine, I've seen so many illusions.... *(To* THE AMANUENSIS*)* Get going. *(Incanting over* THE AMANUENSIS*)* Abandon the preservative chill of this cave, give yourself over to strange, pulsing warmth; the flow of blood, the flood of time, immediate, urgent, like bathing warm in a southern ocean, rocked by currents of another life. All that pain, and thwarted hope, rejected love, grief, disappointment, joy... (THE AMANUENSIS *disappears.*) The heart chases memory through the cavern of dreams.

  It will take a moment for him to cross the threshold. Smoke your pipe, rest your eyes, examine the contents of your purse, or of your soul, or... A moment. And then I think we can begin again.

INTERMISSION

ACT TWO

ALCANDRE: Set the scene, mysterium mechanicum!
The moon, a dead man's pale white eye
Glowers down on your son, doomed now to die....
The night of his destruction creeps towards daybreak,
Shot through with terror, and the whispering breeze
Hissing songs about death through the cemetery trees.
We must begin, begin, begin.

PRIDAMANT: Your spirits seem to lift as my son's fortunes decline.
It's perverse. And insulting.

ALCANDRE: Contradictions accrete, complexities accumulate, I do
love a twist, a succulent complication. I feel positively elated—you
can never tell, when you start these things, how they'll go—say, for
example, that your son had died a day or two after you booted him
out, or say he'd married early, and settled young, in some dull
domicile—a dutiful lawyer, say, how flat, how inelegant that would
have been. But here we have a boy who's a troubling enigma, here
we have a girl with a fierce, conquering heart, here we have a
meddler who's made a mistake—she comes to us now, all riven with
remorse....

(LYSE *appears.*)

PRIDAMANT: And so she should. She's the cause of this grisly farrago;
it's a law of nature I tried to teach him: If you trifle with women you
set their tongues waggling; but my son couldn't be taught, and here
we are.

LYSE: It's a guilty murderer's moon that's rising tonight,
Spreading shadows over graves....
Tomorrow, at dawn,
The murderer dies, my lover, her love — unless....
I have a secret to confess:

I can play,
If I choose, Madam Liberty;
I can, if I want to, set Clindor free.
I know a way to rescue him from death, but
I can't find a way to make myself want to.
Love and hate race after each other,
'Round and 'round
Till not even Solomon could tell them apart;
Indistinct, dangerous, frayed with pain
They riot in my grey and gloomy heart.
Is there no healing for this raw wound,
No shelter from this unforgiving wind,
No release from this life of love and loss?
The night's gone pale with fear of morning,
The setting moon's all undecided—
And before it drops behind the treetops,
A lunatic comes to worship it.

(MATAMORE *enters, bedraggled, furtive.*)

LYSE: Pardon me, Sir...

MATAMORE: *(Terrified)* Aaaahhhh!
The maid! Oh please,
Abuse me not, dread Medusa of the linen closet,
Neither giggle nor sneer, oh dour farouche!
Your laugh might make to marbleize
My much-tormented soul.

LYSE: I'm not in a laughing mood tonight.
What are you doing in Geronte's house,
This late, alone? Where have you been?

MATAMORE: Three days ago there was a ruckus; someone died.
I...I've been in the attic ever since.

LYSE: In the attic! There are rats in the attic!

MATAMORE: Oh, I know, man-sized rats,
My strength from battling them
Is sorely taxed; I thought the house
Would start and wake at the sounds our battle made:
Their screams of rodent agony, my shouts of glory
As I waved my sword....

LYSE: The footman said he heard noises in the attic....

MATAMORE: It was I.

LYSE: He said it sounded like someone weeping.

MATAMORE: It must have been someone else.

LYSE: Who?

MATAMORE: The rats. They wept.

LYSE: Weeping rats?

MATAMORE: Weeping rats; a gruesome sight.

LYSE: You were so frightened by the murder of Adraste
You've spent four days in the attic? What did you eat?

MATAMORE: Kitchen scraps and garbage, stolen at night.
Hannibal, they say, when crossing the Alps,
Would eat the dung of his elephants. So though it was hard
For a man like me to root in the trashheap for mouldy meat,
I knew I was in good company.
And I didn't retire to the attic for fear,
But rather as a place of reflection. I needed time to think.

LYSE: And in these four days, your belly full of garbage,
What conclusions did you reach?

MATAMORE: That this life of love and violence is too much
For a man no longer young.

LYSE: It's wearing hard on everyone;
We're all suddenly growing old.

MATAMORE: But youth has its advantage still—
In these games of passionate exertion
My young apprentice, Delamont,
Has learned so well he far surpasses me.
I never killed a man.
I resign my place to him.
I plan to become a desert monk, a hermit in a cave.

LYSE: There are no deserts in France.

MATAMORE: I thought the moon.

LYSE: The moon?

MATAMORE: Yes, that moon, there.
I've given up hope for this cannibal world;
No good will come of it, or of its creatures,
But ah! the moon....
It's cold and bleak, they say;
Perhaps in a cave, on a comfortable rock,
Viewing the expanse of some lifeless lunar desert,
I'll learn to dream smaller, less tumultuous dreams.

LYSE: If you do learn, come back
And give me instruction....

MATAMORE: I can't, mop-and-bucket;
I'm not coming back. But think of me up there,
My peaceable catechism, draw patient forebearance
From that silvery light.

LYSE: I saw a moon-map once; there's a sea
I remember called Tranquility....

MATAMORE: Yes, yes, I'll find that sea,
Where respite's granted every wanderer
Weary of war, sick of desire....
I'll drink a cup of its water for you.
Adieu, adieu, remember me... *(He exits.)*

LYSE: More than remember: I'll worship you,
My patron saint; you catechize me:
To withdraw my poor heart from the lion's den,
To leave the blood sport of love to my betters.
Want, yes; but Want
Less.
I see a way to a golden means,
By which I am revenged but nobody dies....
I have preparations to make
For an earthbound journey. And yet I will rise
Sky-high, even higher
Than if I followed this man to the moon. *(Exits)*

PRIDAMANT: Narrow the vision, this isn't what I've paid for, you
digress and I want to see Clindor, find out how he's doing—I've
visited prisons often enough, they're terrible places, he's probably
wretched. Show me that.

(ISABELLE *appears, kneeling. Behind her,* THE AMANUENSIS, *dressed as* GERONTE.)

PRIDAMANT: No, no, not the girl, I...

ALCANDRE: Soon, your son, but
First this:
A handsome young woman,
At twilight prayers,
Watched over by her father—

PRIDAMANT: Her father! At last, the father arrives. And now her entreaties will move him to free poor Clindor, and he'll bring it all to a pleasant resolution.

(The hawk's cry is heard again.)

ALCANDRE: Beyond the window, a hawk, as it flies,
Traces in the skies
The jagged edges
Of her broken heart.

ISABELLE: Father, hear me...

GERONTE: Get off your knees.

ISABELLE: If you'll listen, I'll rise.

GERONTE: I cannot hear. I'm deaf as a stone.

ISABELLE: When I was a child, and sick,
My mother used to keep vigil by my bed
All night long.

GERONTE: Yes she did, I remember that. I resented you for it,
Her preoccupation. You always were a troublesome child.

ISABELLE: I'm keeping a vigil
For his deliverance; hear my prayer....

GERONTE: It's very odd; you look like me;
There's a distinct family resemblance, and yet
I can't seem to place you. At times you call to mind
A daughter I once had, sprung from the same
Flinty soil as I, made of fine, tight-woven stuff—
The goblins, I think, stole her away one wild night
And left a changeling in her place, a simpering
Weeping girl, who throws herself at serving-men,

Whose tears are selective, reserved for paupers,
For little ragtag orphan boys....
But she's got no grief to spare, oh no,
For the grotesque murder of a noble young man
Who loved her dearly,
For whose destruction she is not, I'm ashamed to say,
Entirely free of guilt.

ISABELLE: Punish me, then, let me die in Clindor's place.

GERONTE: Oh you'd like that. Whore and martyr, now there's
distinction.

ISABELLE: I am your daughter; if you love me at all....

GERONTE: Love, love, what does love mean?
Nothing! Anything can be called love,
Any ugly emotion—Love, that illusion,
That hydra-headed gargoyle into whose foul maw
Everyone tumbles, giddily, each
With the same insipid look
Of sheeplike expectation.
Love, that sarcophagus,
Love that disease,
That demonic, black misery,
That catastrophe, Love—do I love you?
Oh yes. My daughter. Oh yes I do,
But not like your pauper does, tender and moist,
Not with sweet wet kisses
Tasting faintly of decay....
I love you, Isabelle,
With a heart of ice, drained and dry,
Bred of denial, restraint and control,
A love whose flesh has been boiled off —
A clean cold hard white bonelike love.
I am the Law. Come shiver in my arms.
No? You prefer, of course, your paramour,
His lawless extravagance, his oily heat.

ISABELLE: I'll show you, Father,
How true a daughter of yours I am;
I will become a deadly adversary;

A coiled viper as venomous as you.
I'll give you a hundred hidden reasons to fear me....

GERONTE: Be careful how you threaten:
My patience has its limits.

ISABELLE: Your worst threats hold no terror;
I'd rather you cut my throat
Than kiss my forehead, rather feel
The point of your knife
Than the touch of your hand.

GERONTE: Ludicrous bravado and wasted breath—
Here, my pampered patricide, here:
(He throws his dagger at her feet.)
Murder your father, astonish him,
Show him he was wrong to think you
Feckless, inconstant, weak-willed and flighty....
(He waits for ISABELLE *to pick up the knife.)*
Before his blood's dried on the chopping-block, Isabelle,
You'll have found someone new to amuse yourself....

ISABELLE: Father. Hear me, hear what I pray.
Tomorrow when my lover dies
The world will see your hate triumphant,
A victory of arrant hatred, rank and wealth,
Of sterile men and faceless Law;
I congratulate you for this.
But Father, please know,
The arm that raises the axe tomorrow
Is your arm; the neck on which it falls—
Not Clindor's neck, but mine.
When Clindor dies, I die.
In Paradise we'll be together;
And if you ever loved me,
And my dying brings you grief,
Know, Father, that I mock your sorrow,
That your tears and anguish will bring me
Joy. While you still live, the ghost of me will breathe
An icy cemetery wind through your bones every day,
And in the dark you'll hear me walking about, looking for you.
Every day, and every night;

You'll weep with relief when your last day dawns,
And till you die, I promise, you will envy me my death.

GERONTE: So be it. My daughter. My only child.
His sentence holds. It is the Law. When the sun appears,
He dies. *(Exits)*

PRIDAMANT: It's abominable, isn't it, the way some people treat their
children?

LYSE: *(Entering)* What are you doing there
Down on your knees?
For a mad mad moment I thought
"My God, she's scrubbing the floor!"

ISABELLE: Help me, Lyse.
I can't bear to live
A single instant after he is dead.
(She picks up the dagger.)
Look.
It's my father's knife.

LYSE: Put it away.
There's a less painful solution.

ISABELLE: There's no other remedy.
Assist me or else
Become my enemy.

LYSE: I've saved him.

ISABELLE: Clindor?

LYSE: At liberty tonight.

ISABELLE: Tell me what to do.

LYSE: Meet me at the prison at midnight exactly.
I have the key to Clindor's cell.

ISABELLE: Lyse! How did you get it?

LYSE: His jailer is a lonely man.

ISABELLE: This sacrifice...

LYSE: Is even more than you imagine.

ISABELLE: I swear to you, if he goes free,
You'll live your days a wealthy woman.
I will wait on you.

LYSE: It's not your servitude I crave.
A handsome payment is another matter.
Here are the keys to your father's vaults;
Go in, pack a bag
With all the coins and jewels you can carry.
We flee tonight; you with your love, no longer lonely;
I with the loot, no longer poor.

ISABELLE: I'll give you half of all I have.

LYSE: Only half?

ISABELLE: It's a lot of money.

LYSE: You haven't seen the jailer.

ISABELLE: All then; everything.
You shall have diamonds for setting him free!
Clindor and I will need no gold!
I'll be his equal, we'll both be orphans,
Homeless and poor in the wide, wide world!
How happy we'll be!

LYSE: Both poor. I know Clindor will be overjoyed.

ISABELLE: It's you who deserve this ecstasy, not I.
I am your friend, Lyse, till the day I die. *(Exit)*

LYSE: Tonight when we open the door to his cell
He can claim his newly paupered bride;
I'll have a countinghouse consolation.
I wish them every penniless joy —
I'll jingle money at their wedding.
And how the hungry cat will cry
To find the fattest bird flown away.
Moderation is best, Aristotle said it:
Everyone feasts, but no one is full. *(Exits)*

PRIDAMANT: Well, if the maid is rich, my son's a fool not to choose
her—the other one's a bit high-strung, and likely to be a spendthrift.
On the other hand, the maid's too scheming, it'd be constant work
keeping up with her. I only hope he doesn't make a mistake....

(The scene shifts to CLINDOR'*s cell.)*

PRIDAMANT: Ah! The prison.

CLINDOR: I'm thinking of my father.
When they toss my trunk in the lime pit,
And my astonished severed head in after it,
Will you, father, in your house,
Oblivious, half-a-world away,
Feel some correspondent shiver in your spine?
When the sun and lime have bleached my bones,
Will your mouth, unexpectedly, inexplicably, go dry?
I am the orphan child of fate,
The hero of an old romance....
I think this is the end of me.
I can see the light grow green
And the night recede,
And the footsteps of the guards
As they arrive at my door;
I feel the irons on my wrists and feet,
The weakness in my legs
As we walk down corridors of stone,
The chill of the early morning in the walled courtyard,
The audience at attention, men my father's age,
The hooded stranger with the hand on the handle of the axe
And then....

PRIDAMANT: No...

CLINDOR: My fear's so great I think that I've already died,
And then I wake up, to rehearse it all again.
Why, in the depths of this open-eyed nightmare
Do I cling to a vision of you, Isabelle?
As though you can save me, by returning my love,
As though, wrapped in your love, I can't be killed.
I love you
Isabelle.
I really think that's true....
Oh pardon, spare, forgive, relent,
I don't want to die.

*(*ISABELLE *and* LYSE *enter.)*

ISABELLE: God should not forgive you, my breath, my soul,
But beg your pardon for His villainy.

CLINDOR: This must be some illusion, some tantalizing dream,
Or else some early torment sent
To souls already damned....

LYSE: Not devils, Sir, but
Angels of deliverance, flapping iridescent wings
And rattling keys.

(She opens the door to the cell. ISABELLE runs to his arms.)

ISABELLE: One more day apart from you and I'd have died;
With this embrace we're both restored to life.

CLINDOR: I'm not going to die?

LYSE: Eventually you will, but
Not for years and years.

ISABELLE: When death comes for you, Clindor,
As Lyse is right to say it will,
We two will have grown old and gray together,
Faithful through life, through death,
And till Eternity ends.

LYSE: Yes, and there's no end to Eternity,
Or to Clindor's capacity for love.
Come, before the dawn
Wakes your father from his dreams of execution,
We three must ride
Far beyond the reach of his law and his rage
To a freer, happier, more gentle land....
As we descend on our subterranean voyage,
I'll tell you a tale of the man in the moon....

ISABELLE: Oh yes, Lyse, a story,
A story of love...

LYSE: A story of love...
Very well,
Once there was an orphan;
His father had banished him;
He was very poor;
His lover was wealthy, and she had a maid.

ISABELLE: And through a strange twist of fortune,
The ladies changed places,
And the poor, poor orphan married the one with no money....

LYSE: And the poor, poor maid became very, very rich....

(As they exit, LYSE removes her cloak; she is dressed beautifully. ISABELLE opens her cloak; she is dressed plainly. They laugh, hold hands, and face CLINDOR, who is first bewildered, then dismayed; then he goes to ISABELLE and kisses her. CLINDOR and ISABELLE exit. LYSE is stunned, and then runs after them as she hears the voice of GERONTE.)

GERONTE: Come back! Come back! I banish you forever!
Forever! Forever! Return to me! My gold!
My child! My gold! My child! My gold!
Mine! Mine! All mine! All mine!

(The scene fades to black.)

PRIDAMANT: Thank God that's over. I can breathe again. Light?
Hello?

(Again, the light on THE AMANUENSIS, who is ticking and tocking.)

PRIDAMANT: Yes, yes, I know, time's passing. No need for the reminder. *(Recognizes him)* Ah! It was you! Her father, heartless old Geronte, it was you! That was amazing, you...incarnated him, you did, I've known tight old bastards just like that, I found myself despising you.... Tell me about it, crossing over. Is it as bad as the old charlatan says it is?

AMANUENSIS: It's worse. He doesn't know. He's never been.

PRIDAMANT: He said he had.

AMANUENSIS: He lies.

PRIDAMANT: I thought as much. If you want to get the dirt on someone, make small talk with their servants. You probably never had your tongue cut out or your eardrums pierced, either....

AMANUENSIS: *(Hissing, furious, and very fast, as though pursued)* I did! I do! With a heated razor and bronze needles. You can't imagine what a fiend he really is. How I have to throw myself, again and again when he orders me to, into other lives, full of pain and twisted passion, how many demons are handed me in little bottles with the order, "Swallow this and be possessed!" While baby-fat men like you sit watching, devouring like pigs the agony I produce! Leech men, vampires, you smile, you're sated, you think blood won't call for blood, the crimes you commit are all shellacked, clean and beautiful while your refuse and sewage runs through me like a.... (*He stops in midsentence; his tongue is gone. He puts his hands over his ears; they're deaf.*)

ALCANDRE: Has my servant been amusing? What did he say to you?

PRIDAMANT: I've no idea. He seemed upset about something.

ALCANDRE: Ah, well, he usually is—it's this back-and-forth business, it wears on the nerves. The last vision is ready.

PRIDAMANT: Proceed. The married life of Clindor my son, and Isabelle his wife. I wonder if I have grandchildren.

(HIPPOLYTA *and* CLARINA *appear.*)

CLARINA: This is an endless walk, Hippolyta.
It's taken half the day.

HIPPOLYTA: I need the exercise and air, Clarina; this grove is
A popular place. There's the Palace of Prince Florilame....

PRIDAMANT: I see they've changed the names again. This time I won't let it upset me. It's pleasant to see they've become friends. I had a maid once came into some money, she packed and left without so much as a thank-you-goodbye.

CLARINA: The Prince is away, at sea.

HIPPOLYTA: He's at sea and so am I.
While he's off with his cargo and his ships,
My equally enterprising spouse has been plying
The Prince's wife with merchandise of his own,
Offering her his inimitable protestations of love,
Which she buys wholesale, eager customer that she is.
This forest is their trading post;
They meet here every day, and barter.
I'll walk until that merchant of adultery comes
And then...we'll haggle over prices.
Now you know why I'm here. Keep silent.

CLARINA: I can't. It's you who should keep silent.
Do you think your anger will alter him?
He's had a dozen affairs, and he'll have more,

The more you show him how you're hurt
The more he'll seek them out.

HIPPOLYTA: No, that can't be true.
There must be at least some little soul in him,
Some kernel of human shame he hasn't killed.

CLARINA: I think there was once. He got older.
None of the changes have been for the better.
There's a gradual wearing-down of things.
Accept it. Spare yourself this humiliation.

HIPPOLYTA: Humiliation's all I have Clarina. I revel in it.

CLARINA: You do. The two of you quarrel until you're both hoarse;
You may not have a life together; but this dragon duet
Is only a way of driving each other mad.

HIPPOLYTA: We'll both rave, then. At least I won't be alone.

CLARINA: Well here he comes to keep you company.

HIPPOLYTA: Does he see me? He does. I can't....
Talk to him, please, tell him...

CLARINA: No, this game's best played, I think,
By two, not three, a thing I realized
Years ago. I leave you to your torture;
I've lost my appetite for injury
Through watching how you mull it over.
I'd rather live alone, and so should you,
But you, my poor, poor friend,
Like a beggar, linger outside the almshouse,
Waiting for either a kick or a coin.
Long ago this orphan lost his charm for me,
And I can't bear to watch the way
You beg for the wounds he inflicts.

(CLARINA *and* HIPPOLYTA *run upstage to different corners.* THEOGENES *enters.*)

THEOGENES: Rosine, my own adored,
There's little time for pranks and teasing;
Our tryst today will have to be quick.
My wife's asleep but she'll expect me home....

HIPPOLYTA: *(Turning around)* She knows where to expect you,
Theogenes. And
She's wide awake, though
She seems to be having a very bad dream.

THEOGENES: Oh God...

HIPPOLYTA: In all the worst moments of your life
You make that little gesture and say
"Oh God..." You are the filthiest liar
I've ever met; you can't possibly believe
That God would ever listen to you.

THEOGENES: You're mistaken, Hippolyta, I....

HIPPOLYTA: I was mistaken once; I remember the day,
Though you, I'm sure, don't.
You said you loved me.
I believed you.
I've become wiser,
And now I'm so rarely mistaken
I want to kill myself.
I gave up all the comforts of my father's house
To flee into poverty with you, a common soldier,
Incurred his wrath and broke his heart
And all for what? To stand here trading broken hearts
And tawdry lies with you? If you cannot love me,
Why did you abduct me? And if you will not love me,
And me alone, return me to my father. I'd rather bear
His gloating and contempt and live alone and without love
Than drink this foul-tasting gall of yours.

THEOGENES: You know as well as I your father's doors are barred,
You know his flinty heart won't melt,
Or else you'd have returned a hundred times before,
If your threats mean anything at all.
Go! Live on his doorstep! He may relent, although
If he's a whit like his child he won't.
Like her he has no talent for forgiveness.

HIPPOLYTA: Forgiveness is for people who
Admit that they've transgressed.
How can I forgive you when you swear
You're guilty of nothing at all?

PRIDAMANT: Oh this isn't at all how it should be! They're wrangling like fishpeddlers! Surely after all they've been through they've become more elevated and ennobled!

ALCANDRE: They seem instead to have gotten rather tarnished in the process.

PRIDAMANT: Well I don't like this dissolution. That first vision was the best by far. I'll see if I can remember that and forget the rest of it.

ALCANDRE: Considering what these illusions cost, I can't believe you won't try to retain them all....

PRIDAMANT: I came to you to launder the fabric of my recollected life. You haven't lived up to your promises.

ALCANDRE: I gave you back your son.

THEOGENES: And what have I done? Abducted you?
I abducted *you*? That's a lie; you know Hippolyta
You came willingly enough; your desire for me
Made you accomplice if not mastermind
Of your abduction; you're no victim.
I learned the art of murder for your sake,
And for your sake, I honed my skills
And built a bloody fortune up in service to the prince
To compensate you for your loss of wealth.

HIPPOLYTA: And the prince has amply rewarded your bloody deeds,
And you, in gratitude, no doubt,
Have rendered service to his wife, and she,
Displaying the same fine fealty to the prince
As you her paramour have shown, accepts your servitude;
Once a servant, always a servant; once false, then false forever.

THEOGENES: Oh that's exactly how you women think!
One mistake and everything's ruined,
One indiscretion means a thousand more;
Regardless of the uncountable kindnesses
Your husband may have shown,
The liberty, the veneration,
The indulgence of each weird request;
A husband may be Christlike in his sacrifice to you,
But catch him with a mistress....

HIPPOLYTA: Or two. Or three, or...
How many is it? I've lost count.

THEOGENES: And he becomes the Prince of Darkness in your eyes.
Evil beyond all repair.

HIPPOLYTA: You're not the Prince of Darkness
Or the Son of God. Just something wearily in-between
Hell-bent on disappointing. You keep me around
To forgive you your sins; with each indulgence
Fresh in your heart, you run out
To muddy your soul again
And then back again for more forgiveness.
I'm exhausted by this ritual:
I forgive you for everything, from now
Until the day you die, know that you're in a state
Of Permanent Absolution.
Forget about me, then, and my pardoning,
I'm tired of the subject of myself.
Think of the prince. Surely your benefactor deserves
Better from his favorite than this?
Are you completely lacking in simple gratitude?

THEOGENES: My treason to the prince embarrasses me, but
To be honest, which I'm still capable of being,
In spite of your opinion that I'm not,
There's something in the danger and the treason
I find attractive.
If she wasn't the prince's wife,
I wouldn't want the princess.
Don't forget
The circumstances under which
Our love first caught fire.
Didn't that tell you anything about my tastes?

HIPPOLYTA: I wasn't seeing as clearly then....

THEOGENES: You think that fire's dead.
It still burns furiously. Feel...

(He tries to put her hand on his heart.)

HIPPOLYTA: No... (She touches it.)
The heat's still there, and still impressive;

It's just a trick you learned somewhere,
And meaningless.

THEOGENES: I love you. Allow me this betrayal.
You can find room for my insanity.

HIPPOLYTA: Clarina was right; I must enjoy
Being humiliated or I'd strike you now.
I only ask this:
Consider the danger.
When the Prince learns what you've been doing,
What do you think will happen?
This isn't a game; it's treason, a crime.

THEOGENES: I know; death threatens me for this;
But I've spent my life in love,
And love is all I am; if I cease to love,
I cease to be; I dream of love; I eat love,
Breathe love, bathe my tired heart in love,
Pronounce love over and over and over again till
It sounds like a word from another language,
A word I've lost the meaning for.
How much do you think life really matters
To the creature I've become?
My only hope's that time will wear me out;
My flame will eat up all the air, and die.

HIPPOLYTA: And when your flame's consumed the atmosphere,
What will become of me, do you suppose?
When you've burned up, and all the air is gone,
Do you imagine I'll live on, not breathing?
When we first loved our souls were joined
In joy and bitter struggle both;
We promised an exchange of hearts,
Forever, and, I think, try though you might,
One never does break free of that.
Our lives and deaths are married.
I don't ask you not to die,
But know that when you die,
I also die.

THEOGENES: You only think you will.

HIPPOLYTA: Oh no. You'd understand, my love,
If, after all your talk of love
You understood love at all.

THEOGENES: If our lives and deaths are bound together,
And if, in dying, I would cause your death,
It would also be the case, I suppose,
That you, in living, force me, your friend,
To live.

HIPPOLYTA: Careful logic, well-constructed.
Your reasoning's impeccable.
If you could only promise me....

THEOGENES: I do.
I promise love forever, my single soul,
Complete, eternal, faithful....

HIPPOLYTA: If I could really have that,
For just one simple day,
From the morning till the evening,
Just once....

(THE PRINCE enters.)

THE PRINCE: Ah, Theogenes, there you are.

(HIPPOLYTA and THEOGENES bow.)

THEOGENES: Your Grace! Back sooner than you planned;
Did the weather turn your ship around?

THE PRINCE: A hurricane that blew up unexpectedly
From the Windward Islands;
And troubling news arrived from home.

HIPPOLYTA: I hope your wife, The Princess, is well.

THE PRINCE: Never better. The trouble's small,
A private matter, and easily dispensed with.
I've been hunting.

THEOGENES: I thought I heard your hawk.

THE PRINCE: Mmmm. You probably did. A pity.
This morning, at the hunt,
An archer killed him accidentally.
He served me very well, that hawk.

THEOGENES: That is a pity. Hawks are hard to train.

THE PRINCE: Yes, and rarely worth the trouble.
Too intelligent, too proud. The arrow
Caught him in mid-air; a perfectly-constructed
Thing of flight, in an instant destroyed,
A tangle of broken feathers on the ground.

(THE PRINCE *suddenly draws a knife and stabs* THEOGENES *repeatedly.*)

PRIDAMANT: No! Stop! Alcandre, stop this! He's being murdered!
That man is murdering my son!

HIPPOLYTA: *(Overlapping)* No! Please! Your Grace! Stop! Clarina!
Help! Murder! Murder!

PRIDAMANT: He isn't dead, he isn't dead....

CLARINA: *(Entering)* Oh pity on my soul, Your Majesty, what have
you done?

THE PRINCE: Nothing that the Law would not have done.
My wife, like my crown,
Are cornerstones in the edifice of State.
He should have known better.

HIPPOLYTA: Assassin.

PRIDAMANT: ASSASSIN! MURDERER! Alcandre, turn it back, I...my
heart...

THE PRINCE: Hippolyta, don't anger me.
Justice has been done for you as well;
He never was worthy of your love.

HIPPOLYTA: *(Falling)* I can't breathe,
Clarina, I'm suffocating. *(She collapses; the lights begin to fade.)*

CLARINA: She's fainted. Help me. She...
Oh God, she's cold, like him,
Already dead....

PRIDAMANT: NO! DON'T GO! THIS CANNOT BE! MY SON!

(A great red curtain falls. PRIDAMANT *rushes toward it.* PRIDAMANT *tears down the curtain. There's nothing behind it.)*

PRIDAMANT: Gone...
(He puts his finger to the corner of his eye.)

Look. What is this?
(His finger is wet.)
What's happened to my eyes? Am I bleeding?
No, it's clear, not blood. Some kind of liquid.
(He eats the tear.)
Mmmm. Salty, but quite delicious.

ALCANDRE: Ah. Good. Save a peck for me. *(He goes to* PRIDAMANT, *plucks a tear from his eye, holds it aloft between the thumb and forefinger.)* This, this jewel. This precious leaded crystal pendant. This diamond dolorosa, so hard fought-for, so hard-won, this food, my sustenance, for this infinitesimal seepage, for this atom of remorse, for this little globe, this microcosm in which loss, love, sorrow, consequence dwell in miniature, for this iota, this splintered particle of grief, for this I turn the gumstuck machinery, erect the rickety carpentry of my illusions. For this: to see your granite heart soften, just a bit.

PRIDAMANT: My heart, Magician, doesn't soften, though under considerable duress, it breaks. Scar tissue forms. He's dead. His poor unhappy wife. I'll join him soon. They could have dug a single grave for us both. I never dreamed I'd outlive him. Terrible day, to have seen that.... My eyes hurt, I want never to see again.

ALCANDRE: I have nothing more to show. It's over now.

PRIDAMANT: Finished, yes. It's over.

ALCANDRE: And I'm sure you're anxious to be on your way; at a steady gallop you might make Paris by morning.

PRIDAMANT: Paris? Why on earth would I go there?

ALCANDRE: To...see your son, of course.

PRIDAMANT: To see...? Is he buried in Paris, then?

ALCANDRE: Buried?

PRIDAMANT: I don't want to see his tomb; I hate boneyards, visiting the dead, wax flowers and weeping, it's a ghoulish custom.

ALCANDRE: There seems to be some...misunderstanding here, he's.... Oh my.

PRIDAMANT: Yes?

ALCANDRE: Your son.

PRIDAMANT: What about him?

ALCANDRE: Well—

(Pause; ALCANDRE *looks to* THE AMANUENSIS *for help;* THE AMANUENSIS *only shrugs.)*

ALCANDRE: He isn't dead.

PRIDAMANT: He...I beg your pardon.

ALCANDRE: Your son's not dead, Sir. Not really dead. I merely showed him to you in his present occupation, these...these scenes you watched are from a theatrical repertoire. Scenes from plays. Your son...

PRIDAMANT: Is alive?

ALCANDRE: Is an actor.

PRIDAMANT: Alive?

ALCANDRE: Oh, but yes, alive!

PRIDAMANT: Alive! Alive my son! Alive! I thought....

ALCANDRE: You didn't think this was real? Oh I do apologize for that, Sir, I do, I thought anyone could see.... Oh dear, oh dear, these mooncalves and mockturtles made of illusion and reality, they slip and they slither, I ought to be more careful, more punctillious; really, the distress you must have felt, it's inexcusable.

PRIDAMANT: Where? Where is he?

ALCANDRE: A charming little boulevard theater in Paris near the Tuileries.

(He gestures to THE AMANUENSIS, *who gives* PRIDAMANT *a card with an address.)*

ALCANDRE: Twelve performances a week. Before I sealed myself up in this hermitage, I was frequently in attendance there. But that, ah well that was years ago....

PRIDAMANT: *(Putting on coat, starting to exit)* I can go to him, I can hold him again, kiss him and apologize, beg forgiveness, I can leave behind this void, this cold and haunted emptiness, and clutch him to me, warm and strong and breathing and...breathing...he.... *(He stops in his tracks.)* He's...an actor, you say.

ALCANDRE: He has a promising career.

PRIDAMANT: Then none of his life, this, none of it real, not a fighter, an adventurer, not a pummeler of aristocrats—none of that?

ALCANDRE: No.

PRIDAMANT: No. He's an actor. I don't know that I like that. The theater—all that effort devoted to building a make-believe world out of angel hair and fancy talk, no more substantial than a soap bubble. You are moved at the sight of a foul murder—then the murderer and the murdered are holding hands, taking bows together. It's sinister.

ALCANDRE: Oh not so sinister. What in this world is not evanescent? What in this world is real and not seeming? Love, which seems the realest thing, is really nothing at all; a simple grey rock is a thousand times more tangible than love is; and the earth is such a rock, and love only a breeze that dreams over its surface, weightless and traceless; and yet love's more mineral, more dense, more veined with gold and corrupted with lead, more bitter and more weighty than the earth's profoundest matter. Love is a sea of desire stretched between shores — only the shores are real, but how much more compelling is the sea. Love is the world's infinite mutability; lies, hatred, murder even are all knit up in it; it is the inevitable blossoming of its opposites, a magnificent rose smelling faintly of blood. A dream which makes the world seem...an illusion. The art of illusion is the art of love, and the art of love is the blood-red heart of the world. At times I think there's nothing else. (*Little pause*) My servant has prepared the bill.

PRIDAMANT: I pay bills promptly. I thank you for your services.

ALCANDRE: We try to please our patrons, don't we, my friend?

(THE AMANUENSIS *hands* PRIDAMANT *the bill, glaring at him.*)

PRIDAMANT (*Looking at bill, then looking at card*) My son. I remember the day he was born; I looked at him; this small thing he was. I thought, "This is not like me. This...will disappoint." And you see... I was right. (*Little pause*) I may, if health permits, go to Paris this spring, providing that they've put straw down on the muddy roads and made them passable. It can swallow you up, the mud. Still and all, it might be good to see him again. My son, Theoge... No. His name started with a "C". Crispin? Hmmm... All these memories, and I've forgot his name. (*Exits*)

ALCANDRE: There were heavy rains this February and March. I'd expect a lot of mud. Hah. I am...a tired old fake. Well, goodnight, Dogsbody, make sure the lights are out.

(ALCANDRE *vanishes.* THE AMANUENSIS *begins to lower the lights. When they are suitably dim and theatrical,* MATAMORE *enters.*)

MATAMORE: I want to leave this planet; don't like it here!
Pardon, Sir, can you tell me the way to the moon?
I'm lost and mapless, a wanderer through the world....

(THE AMANUENSIS *points. A huge white moon and stars appear, floating in space.*)

MATAMORE: That way? You're certain of that? Yes,
The road that way seems to be going uphill. *(Exits)*

(THE AMANUENSIS *is alone. He puts a tentative finger in his mouth. The tongue is back. He smiles.*)

AMANUENSIS: Not in this life, but in the next. *(He turns out the lights. End.)*